How To Form a Parish Liturgy Board

Yvonne Cassa
and *Joanne Sanders*

LITURGY
TRAINING
PUBLICATIONS

For David, Matt and Maria,
for Kelly, Tony and Kelly,
whose caring, encouragement and sense of humor sustained us
when otherwise we might have given up.
To you, we dedicate this book with all our love.

We wish to thank Mary Ann Simcoe and Jim Bitney
who helped give shape to this book.

Yvonne Cassa *and* Joanne Sanders

Copyright © 1987, Archdiocese of Chicago: Liturgy Training Publications, 1800 North Hermitage Avenue, Chicago IL 60622-1101; 1-800-933-1800; fax 1-800-933-7094; e-mail orders@ltp.org. All rights reserved.

Design by Jane Caplan.

03 02 01 00 99 98   6 5 4 3 2

ISBN 0-930467-67-1
LITBD

Contents

Foreword

Dear Reader,

In many ways, it is you who brought this book to life. It is you who taught us the need for such a group as a liturgy board. It was you who energized and enabled us to put on paper what is in our hearts.

Since publication of *Groundwork* four years ago, it has been our delight to work in many parishes throughout the Midwest, perhaps even with you. As people shared their stories, we began to see why so many parishes were struggling to have good liturgy. In some situations, education in liturgy has been ignored. Some parishes resisted growth; some lacked openness to lay involvement. But for the most part, the problems were not with liturgy or a shortage of people.

What was lacking for good liturgy was that no one group of people was responsible for it. Where there was a group, it was often weak and had been set up with little or no direction.

This is not really a book about liturgy, but it does presume the reader's sense for liturgy's importance in parish life and a familiarity with the skills and tasks this involves.

This book will help you form and maintain a productive liturgy board. It is based on our experiences in helping parishes.

We believe that when people do their liturgy well week after week they will be people who care for the unsheltered, the hungry, the jobless. They will realize that full, conscious and active participation means more than everyone singing. So we encourage you to make good use of this book.

May you be sensitive to the needs of your assembly as you implement this process. May you be patient with each other and persevere when struggles seem to defeat you. And may God bless your efforts.

With every good wish and many prayers for your success in this project.

Yvonne Cassa
Joanne Sanders

Introduction

Every parish deserves good liturgy. Liturgy is the activity parishes do most in common. It is the activity that builds up the community, enables and celebrates their works. Just because liturgy happens every weekend does not mean that it happens well. Good liturgy happens when a parish takes serious responsibility for it. With only casual attention to liturgy's immediate details, such as scheduling ministers or writing intercessions, an assembly is not likely to have good liturgy. Yet very often such details are the things that define the work of parish liturgy boards. Lacking structures and ministries, committees or boards spend their time planning weekend liturgies. No one is evaluating liturgies or assessing the way liturgy is done in the parish. No one takes responsibility for ministry development or education in liturgy.

Consider the parish where it is three weeks before Easter and the flowers are not yet ordered. Father Assistant calls together two or three trusted friends to plan the Triduum and Eastertime, sew a vestment and work with the lectors. The scenario becomes a familiar one as this group repeatedly rescues the seasons and applies liturgical band-aids. Such a group, anxious as they face the inevitable deadline, can only tend to the most glaring problems. They promise to get an earlier start next time and even to recruit more workers, but somehow those words quickly fade when there is no structure to call forth accountability and realistic expectations.

Still other parishes have some individual—a priest or a lay person—who operates as the Super Liturgist of the parish: writing intercessions, overseeing the placement of every seasonal decoration, meeting with the music groups. When this person is competent, the system can work for a while. Eventually there is disaster. Our Super Liturgist gets ill, moves away, or gives up. If everything has been running smoothly, it will take time before things disintegrate. Even where there are two or three people cementing the liturgical blocks in a parish, can they consistently expend enough energy to sustain good liturgy? The super liturgists and the crisis team both need to expand the ownership of liturgy to include others.

Vatican II has called lay persons to make the liturgy their own. Establishing a productive liturgy board to oversee liturgy is one way to accomplish ownership for our parish liturgies. A liturgy board provides the structure that allows people to define tasks and to discover methods to accomplish them. In this book we suggest a thoughtful, ordered method of forming or reforming a parish liturgy board. The method can be used by beginners or by those who have already made attempts at forming a liturgy board. Whatever your situation, this book offers encouragement and a logical method to help you move from vision to reality. Perhaps you will not need all the steps contained in this book. Work through those steps your parish does need to address and you will develop or reinforce the group's talents and skills. When there are tasks to be done, the necessary structure will be in place to address them.

The process of establishing a liturgy board is a gradual one. If the group is hastily formed without respect both for its own needs and for those of good liturgy, its members may become easily discouraged with the lack of productivity. When a liturgy board must repeatedly address matters of communication and operational procedure, members soon weary. A well-formed board allows for more serious involvement in the way the parish does liturgy.

This is not to say that good organizational development will avoid all problems, tensions and disagreements. But such organization will go far to promote smooth working relationships. Such structure will promote that creativity which cannot happen in crisis. This book will help you build the foundation upon which the creative work of the liturgy—the work of the people—can build.

PART 1:
GETTING IT
TOGETHER

for·ma·tion

THE PROCESS OF FORMING OR PRODUCING

I f any gathering of people is to become an effective work group, the group's purpose must be clear, leadership and structure for its activities must be agreed upon, and methods of working, communicating and decision making must be in place. Of all these things, clarity of purpose is most important.

Some people might initially express the purpose of the liturgy board very broadly: for example, to see that the parish has good liturgy. Although such a purpose may be true, it is too general to be useful. To clarify the purpose, board members must ask: How will this board see to it that the liturgy is good? What is meant by "good" liturgy? What is the board's job description? Who on the board will do what? The board's work is more encompassing than most will see at first. The focus of its work is primarily assessment and making decisions or recommendations for the common prayer of the assembly. Such a board must be pastoral in its operations with members who are formed by the liturgy and educated about the liturgy.

A liturgy board will usually spend much of its time observing what is happening at the Sunday liturgies, discussing these liturgical practices, brainstorming ways to improve what needs attention, and deciding on specific steps to make those improvements. Once change is implemented, the liturgy board is responsible for evaluating the progress and effectiveness of the changes, as well as the response of the assembly to these changes.

In addition to assessment and evaluation, the liturgy board is responsible for the liturgical education of its members, of all liturgical ministers and of the worshiping community itself. The board should also provide direction for those who plan the liturgical seasons, sacramental celebrations, and other liturgical events. The collective efforts of the board members assure the development of all ministries so that liturgy is done well by all who participate.

Because you are reading this book, you see the value in shaping or reshaping a liturgy board. But before embarking on this project, determine if you are the most effective person to initiate it. There are some qualities and attitudes that seem to get the job done. These are often found in complementary personalities of two or more individuals who *work well together.*

Whoever initiates this procedure must firmly believe that liturgy is "the summit towards which the activity of the Church is directed . . . (and) the fount from which all her power flows" (*Constitution on the Sacred Liturgy,* #10). Unless the liturgy is seen as the very core of why we form parish, it is unlikely that the idea of a liturgy board will seem important enough to pursue.

A workable understanding of what is good liturgy is another essential component. This includes knowing the structure of the liturgy, the flow of ritual celebration, and the requirements of good liturgy as outlined in the liturgy documents. Insight into the various liturgical ministries and how they function together is also important.

Anyone working to shape a liturgy board must be comfortable with ritual and aware of how ritual's repetition and rhythm facilitate participation in celebration.

Liturgy board members are ultimately servants of the entire faith community. To be of genuine service, one must know the group he or she is serving: What ethnic groups are represented in the parish? Is there a large elderly population? What are the traditions of the parish? How are people presently participating in the liturgy? Knowing these kinds of things about the parish, its people, and their traditions enables honest assessment of needs and the setting of long term goals for the liturgical life of the parish.

This formation process will require qualities of leadership: the ability to talk to people and to listen to them; the ability to delegate responsibilities; the ability to motivate others; the skill to follow up without checking up; the talent for recognizing people's gifts; the energy to be self-directed.

Whoever takes on this project has to reverence individuality. Diversity will be present in any group and will cause tension. Whether you are establishing a board for the first time or reorganizing your present structure, charity and sensitivity must be dominant.

Whoever seeks to establish a liturgy board must respect the people or structures in the parish. Those persons already in liturgical leadership roles should be involved in the process. This is more than being courteous. It is ensuring that people who have been involved and will be affected are given the opportunity to be part of the process and thus assist with its completion.

The persons establishing a liturgy board must value structure, not for its own sake, but for what it can enable. While a well formed and thoughtful structure is important, its humble and rightful limitations must be respected.

The process outlined here assumes a healthy outlook on what it means to be church. Those establishing the board must have a real desire to see laypeople and clergy work together in harmony.

Shaping or reshaping a board demands an enormous amount of energy. Ask yourself if you and others have the necessary physical and emotional stamina that new beginnings require.

Lastly, a sense of humor, patience, and a strong prayer life are essential. Getting started is not going to be easy. It is worthwhile, important and exciting work, *yes. Easy, no!*

After reading over these qualities perhaps you can visualize yourself with one or two others proceeding with the steps of forming a liturgy board.

If you are not convinced that your parish can take on such a project at this time, if it seems there are other priorities or that resistance would be too great, you might direct your efforts elsewhere temporarily. For example, some of the formative steps, such as empowering ministry chairpersons or providing liturgical education, may precede the development of a board.

Consider another situation. Maybe you picked up this book because you have been the only person holding your parish's liturgy together and you no longer desire such an intense and complex role. Others are not feeling your sense of urgency. You might refuse for now to take on any more responsibilities. Begin to delegate some of the tasks that overwhelm you. At the same time, share your concerns and this book with others until you have a core of interested persons ready to move forward.

In summary, the effectiveness of this process and the ability of liturgy to flourish depend on three things: (1) the emergence of capable people with a common dream; (2) the willingness of those people to give the time it will take; (3) cooperation and respect between and among staff and parishioners. If these three elements are present, the establishment and the ongoing work of a liturgy board are all but sure to succeed.

mod·el

About two weeks ago the liturgy planning team for Christmastime completed their plans and now the liturgy coordinator is following up on various items. The music groups are beginning to rehearse while the environment and art committee is completing vestment and lectionary covers for which they budgeted earlier in the year. And it is only the beginning of Advent at St. Perpetually Ready Parish! Of course, poinsettias and fresh garland have been ordered early to insure the best possible selection and still stay within the budget. The lector chairperson is arranging for the lectors to practice together and give each other support.

Does this sketch of parish worship life seem a bit unreal? Such organization and efficiency is possible. A parish liturgy board that is well structured will be able to get tasks done efficiently without overburdening the members. Careful design, definition of roles, accountability and an appropriate communication network make this happen. When the board is adequately staffed to care for the immediate concerns there will be energy for long-range planning. Some boards are more effective because they pay attention to these essential matters. In this chapter we will explore several models of liturgy boards that work well in various settings.

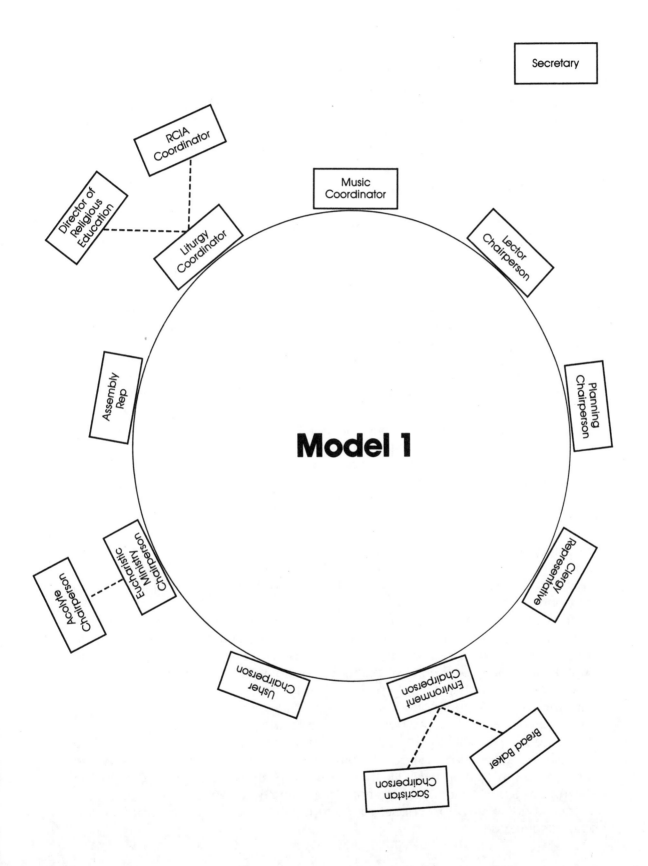

Model 1: The Full Board

The board consists of a liturgy coordinator, a music coordinator, all chairpersons of the primary liturgical ministries, the clergy, an assembly representative and liaisons to related parish groups (such as the catechumenate team and education programs) and the parish school.

The Liturgy Coordinator and the Music Coordinator

The liturgy coordinator, whether full- or part-time, salaried or volunteer, is responsible for those things that enable the work of the other board members. These include: keeping abreast of the ministry chairpersons' progress, affirming what goes well, ensuring that difficulties are addressed, and facilitating goal setting. Essentially the liturgy coordinator ties things together by encouraging appropriate communication between chairpersons and their groups. The coordinator must understand the liturgy, be able to work well with many individuals, and be capable of forming networks with other parish groups. Since this is a very demanding role, this person should ideally be a salaried member of the parish staff. This will depend, however, on the number of people to oversee, the hours expected of the person, and the priorities of the parish budget.

The music coordinator enables the leadership of those who direct the parish music groups and facilitates communication between the liturgy board and music ministers. This person must keep abreast of new developments in worship music to ensure the quality of music at all parish liturgies. Because of the prominence of music in the liturgy and the demanding amount of work needed to maintain that ministry, some parishes find it desirable to hire a full- or part-time music coordinator. When this is not possible, two volunteers may share the job.

Sometimes the roles of the liturgy and music coordinators are assumed by the same individual. This can be effective in a small parish or where lay involvement in liturgical ministry is just emerging. However, combining these roles too often creates an overwhelming workload and results in a less than satisfactory job being done in both areas.

If the budget permits hiring one full-time person, this should be a liturgy coordinator. He or she could assist the volunteer music coordinators as well as provide support in the other areas of liturgy. Another compromise would be to distribute the available salary between two part-time positions: liturgy coordinator and music coordinator. Each job would have a clear focus.

If funds allow for only one part-time staff member in liturgy, this should be someone to oversee the total needs of liturgy in the parish: a liturgy coordinator. When it is not possible to provide any salary for a coordinator, consider inviting the volunteer coordinators to parish staff meetings. This recognizes that they are caring for a vital part of parish life that needs to be represented here. Recognition also means a budget for the coordinator's ongoing education: attendance at conferences and workshops, subscriptions to periodicals, purchase of books and other resources.

Above all, recognize that while a volunteer may be competent, these are demanding positions that call for great energy and a generous gift of time.

In every situation, these positions need the support of the liturgy board members and the parish staff.

Ministry Chairpersons

Each liturgical ministry (lector, usher, communion minister, etc.) is represented on the board so that the needs of all ministers are recognized and addressed. In turn, the presence of these chairpersons on the board helps each ministry define its role in terms of the overall goals set by the board. The ministry chairperson (e.g., usher chairperson) should be a person who excels in his or her particular ministry and who has a solid vision of the overall scope of the liturgy beyond his or her particular ministry. As board members, ministry chairpersons share fully in the work of the board and report to the board on the status of the ministry they represent. (See the chapters on "Job Description" and "Recruitment.")

Clergy

As we attempt to involve the non-ordained in worship ministries, sometimes we forget the role of the ordained. The bishop is ordained to lead the worship of the church. He delegates presbyters (priests) to share in this leadership. In turn, parish priests (pastors and associates) may delegate this leadership to the non-ordained. In a very real sense, a parish liturgy coordinator or other members of the parish staff share in the bishop's own ministry, a "pastoral" ministry.

So the pastor is entrusted by the bishop with the worship life of the parish. Never overlook this responsibility. Any organization benefits when a particular individual can claim, with Harry Truman, "The buck stops here." In practice, someone other than the pastor may be made accountable for parish worship. In any case, it seems fitting that the people who preside over worship should be included on the liturgy board.

Assembly

Every liturgy board needs at least one assembly representative. The *assembly*, after all, does the liturgy. All the ministries serve to facilitate this. The assembly representative is someone who has no investment in a particular ministry, but has the background and ability to offer an unbiased perspective on the total liturgical celebration.

Others

Liaisons with the catechumenate, with religious education, and with any other parish work or ministry that is closely associated with the liturgy should also be

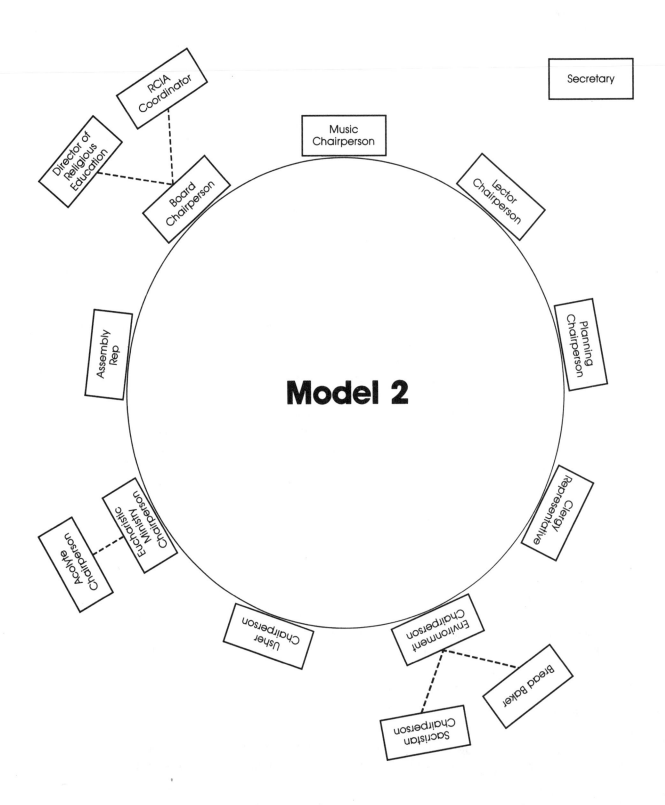

kept in mind in planning for the liturgy board. The directors of these functions may be invited to board meetings as needed for effective coordination of goals and work. They may be liturgy board members if the number of ministry chairpersons is not too large. However, a board with more than nine or ten members will be cumbersome. In a large parish it becomes essential that the board establish ways to be in communication with those whose work is closely related to the liturgy.

Finally, the liturgy board will need to record its activity. Perhaps a non-board member could volunteer to take notes, or the meeting could be taped and the minutes prepared later. Board members need to be free for attentive participation in the work of the meeting.

Model 2: Compromise and Variation

This is a variation that may be necessary when it is not possible to have the desired professionals (liturgy and music coordinators) on the parish staff. This model suffers because the overall concerns of liturgy, the development of the ministry chairpersons, and the many details of liturgical celebration do not always receive adequate attention.

In this model, the chairperson of the liturgy board facilitates board meetings and sets the agenda. Success largely depends on self-motivated, self-disciplined chairpersons and on frequent communication between them and the liturgy board chairperson.

A volunteer chairperson would provide progress reports to the parish council and would be the one to keep a file of the board's activity: minutes from meetings, written policies and budgets, job descriptions of members, yearly goals. The chairperson would be a contact for anyone who needs this information or wants to communicate with the liturgy board.

This model also depends on a strong staff liaison who is concerned for the liturgy and whose job is to devote time to the development of the liturgy board. This is quite different from a member of the parish staff taking on many of the tasks of a liturgy coordinator: problems arise when that person leaves the staff or takes on other responsibilities. A good staff liaison can provide valuable support to the board chairperson and the ministry chairpersons.

There is another limitation to this structure. If liturgy is a "sideline" for everyone—staff and board members—there may be no one at the parish who can stretch the board members and the parishioners to greater insights or ownership of the liturgy.

Model 3: Center Group Plus

Four persons, "the center group," share the responsibilities that would be cared for by a liturgy coordinator. As a group these four engage in long-range planning, evaluation, and other tasks needed to oversee the liturgy. Each individual also

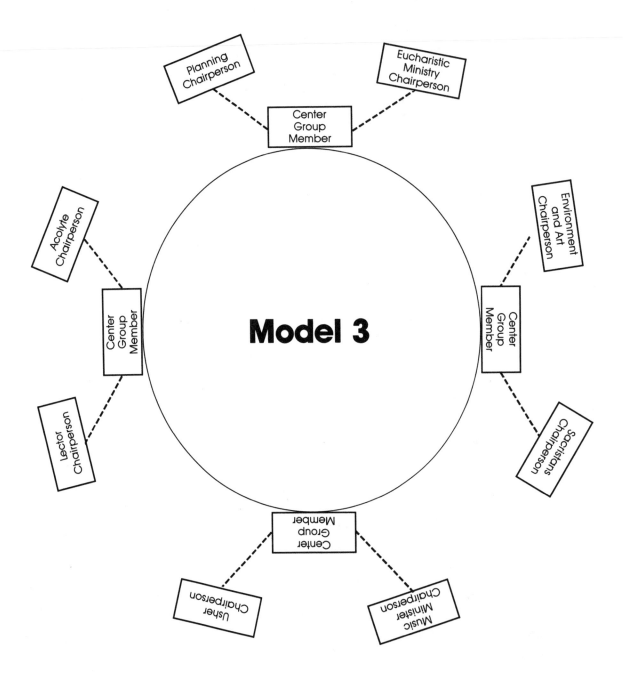

serves as a liaison and resource person to two or three ministry chairpersons or other people with key liturgical roles. In their liaison roles, the center group members provide direction and support to the chairpersons. The center group calls together the chairpersons and any liturgy staff two to four times a year to welcome everyone's input, to provide for education and socializing, and to deepen the ownership of the work of liturgy.

The success of this structure largely depends on the selection of skilled people with a variety of gifts to serve on the center group. Their background should include an excellent knowledge of liturgy as well as strong communication skills. It helps if each center group member has expertise in a different area of liturgy (for instance: music, visual arts). In this way, each ministry chairperson has a resource person who values and understands the contributions of his or her particular ministry to the overall liturgical life of the parish. It is also wise to include clergy and laity in the center group.

This type of liturgy board may be effective, or a good place to start, in:

—a small parish where the operational needs of the liturgy can be handled by a few and the number of liturgical ministers is not great

—a parish with people caring adequately for the liturgical ministries who are able to carry out directives but do not wish to participate in frequent meetings

—a parish that is restructuring a liturgy board after a prior liturgy group "fell apart" and where a few people are willing to oversee the liturgy and rebuild board membership

—a parish beginning to structure a larger board but still in the early stages of recruitment

Conclusion

It is possible to have a board that, on paper, resembles one of these models but still has problems. You may have all the positions filled but you are working on a crisis-to-crisis basis. The board spends time with immediate details and is rarely attentive to the long-range needs of liturgy. Or, your liturgy board may have good representation from the various ministries and job descriptions for each of those positions, but only a few of these people are really working.

In the above situations there is a lack of attention to some of the necessary steps in this process. In the first situation, people were put in place without goals or job descriptions. In the second, it may be that some persons were inadequately trained or that their work had not been evaluated and discussed with them. Closely observe all aspects of your situation before you determine where your problems are and how to proceed.

as·sess·ment

THE ACT OF EVALUATING OR APPRAISING

This section will help you evaluate how liturgy is currently being cared for in the parish and it will help you describe how you would like liturgy to be in the future.

Several people are needed for the beginning steps: assessment, job description and recruitment. These people may become part of the liturgy board, or you may find in recruitment that those who began the process are not the best possible choices or do not want to serve on the liturgy board. Those who get this process started may simply share a vision and have the abilities to choose, enable and empower others.

In assessing the present situation, you may be pleased with the structure in place. It is still important to give attention to the material below, then to proceed to "Job Description," "Procedure," "Budget" or whatever tasks your group needs to address for greater effectiveness. Do not move too quickly to these steps. No matter where you are in terms of structure, you need to articulate as a group (and visually demonstrate) your present situation regarding liturgy. This will more clearly provide direction on how to proceed.

Assessing the Present Situation

As you begin this section, there are two questions to address: (1) Are we meeting the needs of good liturgy? (2) Who is doing the work? Describing the present situation accurately will allow you to determine whether you are sufficiently staffed and are engaged in activities that are properly the work of a liturgy board.

To discover what the parish is doing to meet the needs of good liturgy, we offer the following qualities which define good liturgy: *authenticity, honesty, integrity.*

If liturgy is to be *authentic,* attention must be paid to its roots and traditions as they have been explored and put into books, introductions, rubrics and texts following the directives of Vatican II. Public worship is honest work of the people when it expresses and challenges the faith of the worshiping assembly. The environment, music, objects and gestures must belong to the people. Liturgy is not for spectators. The integrity of parish liturgy refers to liturgy's place within the whole of the community's life. It is not to be an isolated time, but a deed that enlivens all other deeds. Those unfamiliar with these notions should spend time in studying such documents as the *Constitution on the Sacred Liturgy* and *Environment and Art in Catholic Worship.*

In looking at your liturgy, you may want to ask yourself the following questions:

—Have the church's guidelines regarding environment, music, gesture and text been respected?
—Is the ritual a familiar one in keeping with the traditions, one that allows for participation by the entire gathered community?
—Are the liturgical roles exercised by people whose gifts and skills allow for the best possible experience of word, music, prayer?

Assessment: Part One

To assist you in the task of assessment, we include a checklist on "Some Needs of Good Liturgy." This might be given to those involved in the forming/reforming of the liturgy board. Together, the board follows these steps:

Step 1. Ask each person to do *Assessment Worksheet 1.*

Step 2. Next to those things being done, write the names of the people responsible for them. Indicate each person's role in the parish (e.g., lector chairperson, religious education coordinator) even if you do not designate these people as "liturgy board members." Someone, somehow, is giving direction to liturgy in your parish and this needs to be identified and recognized.

Step 3. Sit back and look at your work. Take time to let it sink in. Then invite a discussion of what all this is saying to you. Does it elicit hope, fear, hesitation, excitement, pride? Are there some areas that are receiving a lot of attention and others that are receiving very little? Are there a few people that are doing all the work? Record the comments.

Step 4. If the picture looks confused, or as though there are many things not being attended to right now, that is all right. Continuing to work through this book will help you to draw things into place and gradually incorporate them into your parish's liturgical ministry.

Step 5. Set this work aside, but keep the worksheets posted or keep them for the next gathering if you will not be continuing your work at this time.

Assessment: Part Two

The next step of assessment is to focus on the future, on how you would like the liturgy board to look. This is done by those involved in the forming/reforming of the liturgy board. This is more effective and valuable when done by a group, though some of the tasks will be done individually. This allows for the ideas of each person to surface before reaching consensus.

Each person should envision a model of a liturgy board that would best serve the needs of liturgy in the parish. What positions would be needed to assure that all areas are adequately represented? Each person places the names of positions around their own sheet of paper, called Circle #1.

When everyone has finished, draw Circle #2 on a chalkboard or large poster board. Ask the group to plot out a dream board that represents a consensus of the individual dream boards. Place the names of these positions around Circle #2. Take time with this step, making sure that everyone has a say and that a real consensus is reached. When you have finished, you will have created the desired situation of the group, your parish's ideal liturgy board.

Using another large circle, illustrate your present reality. What kind of structure are you working with? Write around Circle #3 the names of positions that are functioning in your parish at present. Compare your dream board (Circle #2) with your present situation. Discover how many of the positions on the dream board you already have in place. Determine if you have people that are part of your present reality not included in your dream board. Ask yourselves if all areas of liturgy are represented. By too many? By too few? As a group, decide how close you are to the structure you have decided would best meet the needs of good liturgy in your parish.

Once the group has reached a consensus regarding the parish's present situation, you can assess what adjustments need to be made. Discuss the strengths and weaknesses of the structure you now have in place. Assess the possibility of achieving the dream board. Make sure the group considers that achieving its dream board may mean recruiting new people to assure adequate representation, or paring down members to avoid duplication.

Consider whether or not some of the people now caring for some parts of liturgy may be suitable for or want to continue in those capacities. Decide what adjustments need to be made to achieve as much of your dream board as is possible at this time. Using Circle #4, write the names of the positions that represent a feasible liturgy board.

Now it is time for reflection. Sit back and assess the proposed liturgy board as well as the current situation you have collectively described. Make sure the group addresses the following questions:

—Are the people presently involved in parish liturgy helping to achieve the liturgy we desire for our assembly?
—Do the leaders of the liturgical ministers have the skill and talent necessary to do the work of the board?
—Does the present group feel comfortable with the things they are doing now? Are there other areas that need to be addressed?
—If change is needed, does our dream board assure us of this change? Does our feasible board assure us of this change?

After you have gone through and discussed these questions, take time to read through *Assessment Worksheet 2.* Use the components listed on the worksheet to assess what you have in your present reality and in your feasible model. In your present reality, it is likely that some of the components may not be there. Be sure to ask yourselves if the model you consider feasible improves your situation. Continue to review those components when you form your final structure.

Assessment is so important because no matter what your current structure looks like or how you would like it to be, those involved in this process will need to determine what is suitable and workable for your parish. Your liturgy board need not be a replica of the sample boards that we described earlier. However, experience would indicate that the components listed on *Assessment Worksheet 2* are essential for any style of liturgy board.

Assessment Worksheet 1
Some Needs of Good Liturgy

Liturgical ministers

eucharistic ministers	sacristans	presider	cantors
greeters	artisans	lectors	servers
gift bearers	bread bakers	musicians	others

Which of these ministers do we have?

For which do we have initial training?

For which do we have ongoing formation?

For which do we have evaluation?

Indicate strengths and weaknesses in these areas. This is not an exhaustive list. Add appropriate areas.

—quality liturgical objects, vesture

—environment and art appropriate to the liturgical season

—good proclamation

—a worship space that has been given careful attention

—graceful movement and gesture

—music appropriate to the liturgical season

—music suitable for the worshiping assembly

Assessment Worksheet 2
Essential Components of a Liturgy Board

Read each of the following components. Indicate with an X whether you currently *have* or *still need* to work on acquiring each component.

1. An avenue of communication between the board and each ministry.
   Have_____Still Need_____

2. A staff liaison. Have_____Still Need_____

3. A provision for regular meetings (times and places). Have_____ Still Need_____

4. A process for decision making acceptable to everyone.
   Have_____ Still Need_____

5. Enough people to get the job done. Have_____ Still Need_____

6. A fair division of labor and shared sense of ownership. Have _____ Still Need_____

7. A focus for work clearly based on liturgical concerns and on serving the assembly.
   Have_____ Still Need_____

8. General enthusiasm. Have_____ Still Need_____

9. A spirit of cooperation and mutual respect. Have_____ Still Need_____

10. Concern for and involvement in self-evaluation. Have_____ Still Need_____

job de·scrip·tion

Now that you know who you would like to see on the liturgy board, it's probably time to begin looking for people to fill those positions, right? Wrong! There is a prior step to recruiting: preparing job descriptions for the liturgy board members, for ministry chairpersons, for any paid or volunteer positions. Even if a liturgy board or ministry chairpersons are in place and getting their jobs done without the benefit of a job description, preparing one now can clarify those jobs and simplify future work.

Job descriptions for those who carry out the work of the liturgy enhance their effectiveness and direct their tasks. Such descriptions specify enough so that everyone is clear about the responsibilities and authority identified with a given position, especially the person who holds the job.

A useful job description will:

—provide clear expectations of the job
—be the instrument to guide recruiting for the job
—eliminate unnecessary duplication of tasks
—become a basis for supporting comments on annual evaluations
—tell the "what" of a particular job and leave the "how" to the person doing the job.

The last point is worth exploring further. A job description gives enough information to clarify what

AN ACTION
THAT NEEDS TO
BE DONE;
THE ACT,
PROCESS OR
TECHNIQUE OF
DESCRIBING

the job is about and yet allows room for the person to develop the job according to her or his own style of working. For example, the lector chairperson may be responsible for scheduling lectors. This may be done by meeting with the lectors, by letter or phone, by delegating that particular task to someone else. People are likely to be more efficient when allowed to work in the style most comfortable for them.

Components of a Job Description

The following must be included in any job description:

1. Job title: a descriptive name which best identifies the function of this particular job.

2. Accountability: To whom does the group or person holding the job report?

3. Qualifications or special requirements for the job: What qualities or skills will be needed to do the tasks?

4. Overall responsibility or purpose: Summarizing or grouping the job's duties will help in arriving at such a statement.

5. Who benefits from the job? In the case of liturgy, part of the answer to this must always be stated in terms of the assembly.

6. Specific duties: These are often found by brainstorming what someone in this position needs to do. As you list each of the tasks or duties of the particular job, begin with a verb such as "promote" or "sponsor" to clearly define the action.

7. Time commitment: Estimate as closely as possible how much time is required to do this job.

8. Length of commitment: Specify when the job will be reviewed and updated.

Arriving at a Job Description

To arrive at a job description begin by gathering as many facts as you can about the job. Put this information on a copy of the Job Description Worksheet; this is a data collection sheet, your "scrap paper" as you begin your work. Then translate these facts into a formal job description. Two samples of such a description are given at the end of this chapter. From these, devise your own form for job descriptions. On such a form, then, put in good order those things you noted on each data collection sheet. In doing this, always begin by determining the "specific duties." Once they are firm it will be easier to discover the overall purpose, qualifications, time commitment, etc. If the job description is formed in this way, everything that needs to be included will be addressed and each step of the worksheet will give direction to the next. It is important to keep in mind that the "duties" are specific but they do *not* describe the way something is to be done. It might be the duty of the music chairperson to see to the recruitment and training of cantors, but that is as far as the job description should go. It should not try to specify how cantors are recruited or trained.

Arriving at a Liturgy Board Member's Job Description

Some of this work has already been done in "Assessment." Refer to those work-sheets to help you fill out the *Job Description Worksheet.* The needs of good liturgy will suggest input for some of the building blocks that make up this data collection sheet. If good liturgy needs educated ministers, this will be one of the duties of the liturgy board. If it is important to good liturgy that evaluation take place, this has to be included in the work of the board. Recast the data into a job description, beginning with specific duties written in the style suggested earlier. For example:

1) Provide education for the board members, liturgical ministers and the assembly.

2) Evaluate the weekend liturgies of a liturgical season.

A sample liturgy board member's job description is given below. Notice that several of the duties do not refer to areas of work in liturgy. Instead, they are matters that are appropriate to the maintenance of the board. The items in this category include recruiting members, preparing a budget and evaluating the structure and function of the board.

Refer to the data collection sheet and the list of duties to help you decide the necessary qualifications of a liturgy board member. For example, if one of the duties is evaluation, what would qualify a person?

Arriving at a Ministry Chairperson's Job Description

Use a copy of the *Job Description Worksheet* for each ministry chairperson's job description. You will notice that the same items will occur over and over in various job descriptions. That is to be expected. Other duties will be particular (for example, the music chairperson will know how to arrange copyright permissions). The purpose of each job will be specific, expressing the way that the job serves the prayer of the assembly. In models one and two, each ministry chair-person on the board always has two job descriptions: first, a job description as a liturgy board member; second, a job description for chairing a particular ministry.

Job Description Worksheet
Data Collection Sheet for Shaping a Job Description

(This sheet can be used to prepare any job description.)

Job title:

What is the purpose of the job in broad terms? Indicate whom this service/job benefits.

How does this job support the work of the liturgy board/the parish's liturgical needs?

What are the duties of this position? (Use simple language.)

What skills and talents are needed for this position?

What knowledge is necessary for this position?

What kind of time commitment is expected?

What is the length of commitment?

To whom is this person accountable?

Sample Job Description

TITLE: Liturgy Board Member
ACCOUNTABLE TO: Parish Council
QUALIFICATIONS/SPECIAL REQUIREMENTS OF THE MEMBERS:

—Knowledge of liturgy basics or willingness to be trained in this area

—Leadership abilities or willingness to be trained in this area

—Basic sense of ritual celebration

—Prefer current involvement in liturgical ministry

LENGTH OF COMMITMENT: Two years with annual evaluation; three years maximum.
TIME COMMITMENT: Six hours per month (may vary depending on the liturgical season or project).
RESPONSIBILITY: Promote programs of education, liturgy planning, ministry development and evaluation to help develop the liturgical life of the parish; make decisions according to Vatican II liturgy documents.
DUTIES:

Primary: these elaborate on overall purpose and responsibility

1. Provide education for the liturgy board, ministry chairpersons, ministers and the assembly.
2. Identify the liturgical needs of the parish.
3. Set goals and objectives.
4. Evaluate liturgical seasons and Sunday liturgies.
5. Define the board's work according to the parish mission statement.
6. Provide support and appreciation for the board and liturgical ministers.

Secondary: these keep things going

7. Recruit additional/replacement members for the liturgy board.
8. Determine policies and procedures for the board.
9. Prepare a yearly budget for the board and for all the liturgical works of the parish.
10. Provide spiritual growth opportunities for the liturgy board.
11. Review the structure and function of the board annually.
12. Keep accurate records of expenditures.
13. Keep records of meeting activity.
14. Assist in the hiring of staff in the area of worship.

Other: these allow for integration and communication

15. Attend regular and required meetings.
16. Report to the parish council.
17. Communicate with chairpersons of other parish organizations and staff.
18. Be available to parish organizations for assistance in planning and assessing various liturgies/sacramental celebrations.
19. Cooperate with and participate in diocesan, community and parish functions where appropriate.

Sample Job Description

TITLE: Lector Chairperson

ACCOUNTABLE TO: Liturgy Board

QUALIFICATIONS/SPECIAL REQUIREMENTS:

—Two years experience as a lector

—Excel in proclamation of scripture

—One year background in liturgy or willingness to be involved in educational program in field of liturgy; continued education in this ministry on a yearly basis

—Past supervisory experience

—Organizational and communication skills or willingness to develop these skills

LENGTH OF COMMITMENT: Two years with annual evaluation.

TIME COMMITMENT: Eight hours per month.

RESPONSIBILITY: Oversee the recruiting, training and maintenance of the lector ministry of the parish so that the assembly experiences good proclamation. Serve as a liturgy board member, functioning as a representative of lectors and as an active participant in the work of the liturgy board.

DUTIES:
1. Recruit additional/replacement persons to the lector ministry.
2. Provide initial training for lectors.
3. Provide the necessary tools needed for preparation and proclamation of the scriptures.
4. Maintain and distribute a current list of lectors.
5. Be responsible for scheduling lectors.
6. Provide ongoing training for lectors through articles, tapes, workshops, books, etc., on a yearly basis.
7. Affirm and support lectors in their ministry.
8. Evaluate the performance/abilities/needs of lectors.
9. Develop a yearly budget for this ministry.
10. Keep accurate records of expenditures.
11. Conduct meetings for lectors.
12. Communicate as necessary with other parish chairpersons and staff.
13. Serve on the liturgy board.
14. Act as a liaison between lectors and the liturgy board.

re·cruit·ment

TO

SUPPLY WITH

NEW MEMBERS

OR EMPLOYEES

Once you know what you are asking people to do and have clearly defined the work of the liturgy board through the job description, it is almost time to begin recruiting. But first it is important to reflect on your attitudes toward volunteers.

Most of the people who are recruited for liturgy boards are volunteers. Too often we hear complaints about poor work done by volunteers: "But what can I do? He's a volunteer!" We need a more informed attitude toward volunteers and a more enlightened approach to their recruitment, placement and training. Many organizations that rely on volunteers to achieve their mission—hospitals, Parents Anonymous, hotlines, etc.—see to it that volunteers are interviewed, placed according to their suitability for the job, and adequately trained.

Careful recruitment avoids setting up volunteers for failure and avoids frustration for those who work with them. Not only is the parish likely to receive the competent service it deserves, but the volunteers will clearly know the nature and demands of the job and have a reasonable expectation of enjoying success. Volunteers want to spend time and energy in a place that will count. The recruitment techniques described here support this kind of care for the quality of service given by our valued volunteers.

Personal Needs and Qualities

In developing job descriptions you named the prerequisite areas of knowledge and skills for each job. Before recruiting, it is also helpful to identify the *personal* qualities that are desirable in those who serve as board members and ministry chairpersons. The fact that this service will take place in a church setting will help you to determine these preferred attributes or qualities.

Further, it is reasonable to expect a certain degree of emotional health in board members and other key people, especially those who oversee the work of others. Some people seek membership on church committees to find a degree of belonging and acceptance that they have not found elsewhere. The desire to belong to something is one of the primary, healthy reasons for joining any group, but if the liturgy board—or any volunteer position or committee—is the principal place a person expects to fill the need for acceptance, the board is headed for trouble. Board members should be able to expect their contribution to be valued, but this group is not designed only to meet personal needs. There is work to be done! The same is true of finding a place to exercise influence and make a difference. Having a role on the liturgy board can certainly meet these needs; this, too, is a familiar reason for joining an organization. And, if the board is functioning well, every member should be able to contribute to the life and direction of the liturgy. But it is also possible that someone's need to control the group can be extreme.

Other qualities may be desirable in those who are entrusted with leadership and direction for the liturgy; others may be added. Board members are people who:

—have a healthy outlook on the church
—are able to work with and value the contributions of both clergy and laity
—support liturgical restoration and renewal
—are not on a crusade to change the parish (but never eliminate people with new and fresh ideas!)
—are open to learning and to change
—will collaborate with others, lead when they are in charge, and follow when appropriate
—have the time to devote to the work

To summarize, exercise responsible judgment in recruiting and accepting the services of volunteers. This can sometimes mean waiting for the best possible person before filling a position. This is a better course than getting a willing soul who is unable to do justice to the job.

Steps in Recruiting

There are five steps in the recruitment process:

1) surfacing names of potential members

2) deciding whom to invite
3) inviting people to interview for the job
4) interviewing
5) the selection

In the following description, we will focus on recruiting board members, but the same steps apply to any recruiting.

Surfacing Names

In whatever scenario you find yourself—creating a new board or replacing one or two members—you will want to rely on active ministers, parish personnel, and others who can assist you in surfacing names. In some cases there are ministry chairpersons in place but they have never been invited to be part of a board. Here you need to decide if these people are suitable candidates for board members. Do they even want to be considered for membership? What if they do not want to interview for the position or if they do not seem qualified to be part of the board? You may then need to surface names for those positions, too. Or, if the existing ministry chairperson is effective in many ways, you may suggest that this person delegate the responsibility of board membership to a capable minister. This is one style of job sharing.

One way to ascertain the strengths or potential of an individual is by looking at his or her jobs, hobbies and interests. Someone involved in art or design may be able to apply those skills to the position of environment and art chairperson. Someone in a managerial position who is accustomed to overseeing the work of others, communicating and organizing might be an excellent member of the "Center Group" in the "Center Group Plus" example of a liturgy board.

To get information about parishioners' jobs, hobbies and interests, find out if parish census or registration data is available to you. Observation is another excellent resource. Pay attention to what people are involved in, notice what they do well, observe what kinds of activities they usually participate in and the skills they enjoy using. You can also get to know people's strengths and interests by talking with them or with others who know them or who have worked with them.

Everyone working on the name-surfacing phase of recruitment should first review the job description for the position(s) that needs to be filled, and then come up with a list of people who might be likely candidates for that role. This can be done in one meeting if there are only one or two positions to fill. It could require more time and some preliminary work if several positions are open.

If you can't come up with anyone to fill a particular position, ask yourselves why not. Has there been inadequate training in that ministry so that no one excels in it? Has there been leadership formation? The answers to these questions may give the board things to work on once it's formed. You may need to look outside the existing group of ministers, perhaps to some one who previously served in that ministry. You may need to recruit new ministers and develop their leadership before finding a chairperson. It is better to have no one in the position for a while than to have a poor leader. In surfacing names, remember that someone presently heading a particular ministry or already serving on the liturgy board as a member-at-large may be better suited to lead in a different area of ministry.

Deciding Whom to Invite

For each position, begin by listing on a large sheet of paper or blackboard all the possible candidates without comment or discussion. This encourages everyone to contribute without judgment and prevents closing off the topic without having explored the possibilities fully.

Once you have a list of possible candidates, each person should be considered honestly and in terms of competence, not in terms of popularity. Such discussion must remain confidential. During the discussion remember that group members may have different priorities when considering a particular individual or position. For example, one person may feel that the most important duty of the position is scheduling ministers while another thinks providing training is most essential. Therefore, those involved in this appraisal need to be clear about the most important element(s) of a particular job description and the essential qualities needed by a candidate for that position. By reaching a consensus on these matters the group can narrow the list to the two or three best possible choices for the job.

If it is difficult to compare and eliminate names of candidates who are very similar in ability, consider the following as you weigh your choices:

—Is he/she a leader?
—Is he/she able to collaborate with others?
—What is his/her level of competence in the particular ministry?
—Is he/she likely to have adequate time for this job?
—Does he/she exhibit emotional well-being?
—Does he/she have support from friends, family, other interests?
—Is he/she capable of the broad vision it takes to serve the whole community, or might the person primarily want to serve his or her own agenda?

Inviting People to Interview for the Job

After deciding the names of candidates, invite them to interview for the position(s). The style of invitation contributes greatly to a favorable response. An invitation needs to be intentional, attractive and sensitive. If you write a letter, clearly communicate what you are inviting the person to do, why you believe he or she is suitable, and what will be the follow-up (see *Sample Letter of Invitation*). A letter allows the person some time to consider the offer. Then follow up with a phone call or visit about one week later to discuss the person's response. Remember, at this stage of recruitment you are inviting someone to an interview, not to a position.

In your first encounter, let the person know that he or she is being considered for the position and briefly describe what the position entails. Do not ask the person to respond immediately. Rather, ask that he or she reflect on what you have proposed, and say that you will be in touch again in about one week. This avoids putting someone on the spot. If you receive a favorable response, set up a time for an interview and send the person a copy of the job descriptions for a board member and ministry chairperson if appropriate. Include a copy of the *Volunteer Information Sheet* for the person to fill out and bring to the interview.

Fill out a copy of the *Invitation Worksheet* for each position needed. This sheet will not only help you keep a list and a record of the people invited, it also enables you to decide who will do the inviting and interviewing, and it helps you to retain an accurate timetable of the inviting and interviewing process. The *Sample Invitation Worksheet* will help you as you fill in your own worksheets.

Interviewing

While the business world and most volunteer organizations recognize the need for interviews, the church has tended to accept whoever was willing to do the job. In most cases, it mattered little if the person was the right choice. If the person was willing, he or she was in. Today, however, we realize that such methods do not best serve anyone. Thus, it is important that you work hard to match the best possible person with the job that best suits him or her and the community as a whole. Such sensitivity contributes to good liturgy in the parish setting. To accomplish all this, choosing a liturgy board member, a ministry chairperson, and/or a specific minister must begin with an interview. Remember, this interview is always rooted in the job description, which tells the prospective member what you are looking for, and which enables the interviewer to formulate good questions.

Conduct an interview with a single interviewer. A group of interviewers tends to overwhelm. If a new liturgy board is being formed, it makes sense for a staff member (pastor, associate, etc.) to handle the interview process. If a parish already has a board, the liturgy coordinator, the chairperson of the board or the ministry chairperson would be good choices. Be sure to draw on the talents of any board member with competence in the interviewing process.

The individual doing the interviewing needs to prepare for this important task. The interviewer begins by carefully going over the position's *Invitation Worksheet* and the job description. The interviewer will rely on the latter to tailor interview questions that reflect the position's most important duties and that will help surface the candidate's ability—and suitability—to perform those duties. The interviewer needs to ascertain which qualities are essential to the position and which are extra benefits. For example, one may prefer to select as a board member someone who has had extensive training in a particular ministry (an extra benefit). However, one might also be quite satisfied with a candidate who is interested and willing to pursue training opportunities (essential quality).

Provide a suitable environment for the interview. Choose a hospitable place that invites conversation. It can be less threatening to both if the place is "neutral turf." Avoid sitting behind a desk or anything else that sets up a physical barrier between interviewer and candidate. Meet in a warm atmosphere, perhaps over a cup of coffee or tea. Once these preparations are made, you are ready to conduct the interview.

The interview itself should take no more than 20 or 30 minutes. During that time, the candidate should do most of the talking. Since you will not be able to remember every detail of your conversation with the candidate, take notes. At the beginning of the interview, be sure to explain this to the candidate and to tell him or her why you are doing it. Use a copy of the *Interview Worksheet* to assist you in the note-taking task. (See also the *Sample Interview Worksheet* for a completed example of interview note-taking.)

The interview itself should be conducted in three parts: (1) introduction; (2) body; (3) closure. In the introductory period, provide a warm welcome and engage in some informal conversation.

In the body of the dialogue ask open-ended questions. Be prepared to cover the key concerns of the particular position. Open-ended questions require a thoughtful answer rather than a simple yes or no. "What do you like best about ushering?" is better than "Do you like being a usher?" The first question provides more insight into the person's feelings and attitudes. When possible, explore the candidate's behavior in other volunteer experiences, since people often tend to repeat patterns. However, successful involvement in another experience is not always a good indicator of one's ability to serve on a liturgy board. Explore any potential you may suspect and avoid making hasty assumptions. Where necessary, use good clarifying language: "What did you mean when you said you enjoy organizing projects? Can you give me an example?" Also, probing questions/statements are helpful when an answer is unclear: "It would help if you would tell me more about your volunteer work at the hospital."

The last part of the interview is closure. It is important to bring the discussion to a comfortable conclusion and to let the person know when he or she will hear next from you. Ending on a cheerful note and following through on your promised contact is essential.

At the end of this chapter, you will find a listing of *Sample Communication Skills* as well as a *Sample Interview Dialogue* that may prove helpful as you prepare to interview candidates for your liturgy board.

The Selection

After the interviews are completed, the group should meet and review the notes from the interviews. The *group* will make the final decision on who will serve on the liturgy board. Remember, be selective. Choose those candidates who seem best qualified and suited to the purpose of the board. It is a serious responsibility to oversee the liturgical life of the parish. In going through the selection process you will again want to have the job description(s) at hand and be clear on what factors are most important, as you did in surfacing names. Be certain that everyone understands that these discussions must be marked by confidentiality.

The final step of recruitment is the actual empowerment of the selected candidate(s), at which time the details of his or her responsibilities are outlined—in other words, firming up the job description.

You are now well on your way to having a fine and spirited board. These first steps—assessment, job description and recruitment—can be hard and tedious work at times. Nonetheless, those who successfully complete these steps will find the remainder of the liturgy board formation process much easier.

date(s), at which time the details of his or her responsibilities are outlined—in other words, firming up the job description.

You are now well on your way to having a fine and spirited board. These first steps—assessment, job description and recruitment—can be hard and tedious work at times. Nonetheless, those who successfully complete these steps will find the remainder of the liturgy board formation process much easier.

Invitation Worksheet

For what position are we presently recruiting?

What are names of the prospective choices?

What methods of invitation will we use? (Consider what has worked well in the past; consider ways we have not tried.)

Who will do the actual inviting/follow-up? (Consider who is available. Who has the best skills in the method described above?)

Who will do the interview process? (Consider who is available. Who has the necessary communication skills?)

Possible Schedule:

Invitation_____   **Follow-up**_____

Interview_____   **Selection**_____

Sample Invitation Worksheet

For what position are we presently recruiting? Lector chairperson

What are names of the prospective choices?

Bob Jackson

Elaine Reynolds

What methods of invitation will we use? (Consider what has worked well in the past; consider ways we have not tried.)

Send letter

follow-up with phone call

Who will do the actual inviting/follow-up? (Consider who is available. Who has the best skills in the method described above?)

Joyce Swanson

Who will do the interview process? (Consider who is available. Who has the necessary communication skills?)

Joyce Swanson

Possible Schedule:

Invitation _____Aug. 5_____   Follow-up_____Aug. 12_____

Interview__Aug. 15-20__   Selection__Aug. 25__

Sample Letter of Invitation

Dear Stephanie,

Here at St. Perpetually Ready, our parish worship requires the gifts and contributions of many. To serve the prayer life of our faith community, Pastor Smith, Michael Stein and myself are beginning to build membership on the parish liturgy board. This board would oversee the common prayer of the parish. We especially need someone from the lector ministry. Your contribution to this ministry is valued and recognized by those of us working on forming the liturgy board. Because of your excellence as a lector and the concern you have expressed for the liturgy, we invite you to interview for this role of lector chairperson and member of the liturgy board. In the next week, I will be calling you in the hope that you will agree to discuss what serving on the liturgy board would mean. Prior to the interview, we will furnish you with job descriptions that better explain what the role involves and what we hope to be about in the parish.

In closing, I thank you for your fine proclamation of the Word and ask that you consider this invitation thoughtfully and with prayer. Looking forward to talking with you next week.

Sincerely,

Anna Magnani

Volunteer Information Sheet

Please fill in the following information.

Name: _____

Address: _____

Phone: home: _____ **work:** _____

Present ministry involvement:

Past ministry involvement (in this parish/elsewhere):

What training (formal/informal) have you had in liturgy, leadership, communication skills?

Present employment:

Brief employment history:

Other volunteer involvement (present/past):

Hobbies, interests, etc.:

Interview Worksheet

Person interviewed:

For what position:

Interviewer:

Date of interview:

Background information including why this person seems qualified:

Strengths/weaknesses based on job description(s):

Other remarks of the interviewer:

Sample Interview Worksheet

Person interviewed: Elaine Reynolds

For what position: Lector Chairperson

Interviewer: Joyce Swanson

Date of interview: Aug. 18

Background information including why this person seems qualified:

B.A. in English/extensive theater background/good lector — has been one for approx. 2 years/ has faithfully attended all lector workshops/ is a member of the Bible Study Group.

Strengths/weaknesses based on job description(s):

Willing to learn about liturgy; strong feelings about good proclamation and the lector ministry; good organizational skills; has not had an opportunity to take classes on communication skills; very involved in community theater which could create a time conflict.

Other remarks of the interviewer:

Although Elaine has not assumed leadership roles, she is bright, outgoing and seems to be well liked in the parish. She is eager to learn and open to new thoughts.

Sample Communication Skills

Door-openers:

—"Tell me more."

—"I'm interested in what made you first consider this ministry."

Open-ended questions:

—"How have your past experiences prepared you for this position?"

—"What strengths would you bring to this position?"

—"In what other situations have you functioned in a leadership role?"

—"What workshops have you attended in the area of liturgy?"

—"What do you think you will like best about being part of the liturgy board?"

Clarifying statements/questions:

—"I'm not sure I understand what you meant by overseeing the candy stripers."

—"Are you saying that you're disappointed in the way lectors are being scheduled?"

—"It seems as though you are saying that you prefer working in a small group."

Probing statements/questions:

—"What did you mean when you said you were in charge of the library volunteers?"

—"What specifically did you contribute to the planning of the parish's centennial?"

—"Tell me more about the work you did in the theater."

Questions to be asked of any prospective liturgy board member:

—"Tell me how you see the role of liturgy in the parish."

—"What have been your duties in other parishes?"

—"What has been your experience in supervising or overseeing others?"

—"What do you think would be your greatest strength as a liturgy board member?"

—"Do you have any questions about the liturgy board here at St. George's?"

—"What are your thoughts about making a two-year commitment to the board?"

—"How would you feel about attending training sessions to prepare for the work of the board?"

—"Have you attended any liturgy workshops, conferences, or read any books or articles on liturgy?"

—"From your own experience, what do you see as the necessary qualities of a good leader?"

Sample Interview Dialogue

I = Interviewer
C = Candidate

I: What has been your past experience in working with church environments?

C: Well, back in college I helped out with liturgy at the Newman Club.

I: Tell me more about that.

C: O.K. I did the floral arrangements for Christmastime and Eastertime, and, oh yes! I helped design banners. Of course, back then we added words to everything—the more on the banner the better. But recently I attended a workshop on the arts and now I see things differently.

I: What do you mean by differently?

C: Well, let's see—I've learned that wordiness can distract the people, and it can be better to stay with some simple symbol, abstraction, or just color can set the mood.

(So far we have discovered that this person has some background in liturgy, has some degree of openness, was willing to listen to new ideas, and was willing to go to a meeting and learn more.)

I: I see here on your Volunteer Information Sheet that you lived for awhile in another parish. What was your involvement in liturgy at that parish?

C: Oh, I worked on the Environment and Art Committee, implementing the suggestions of the planners, as well as designing and placing things tastefully.

I: What do you see as your greatest strength in the area of art in liturgy?

C: I seem to have a real eye for putting things together—floral arrangements and grouping objects together in a pleasing form—that kind of thing.

I: Have you received any liturgy training in the liturgy documents?

C: I haven't actually taken a course on the documents as such, but I did attend a conference, which was specifically on environment and art. Most of what I've learned has been on-the-job training.

I: If you became a member of the board, we would expect you to attend several training sessions. What would you think about that?

C: I would enjoy updating my knowledge and being with the other people on the board. I think it would be a great way to start out as a group. However, I would be concerned about having to travel far for this training, especially at night.

Sample Interview Dialogue, continued.

(This seems to be a person with a high degree of openness and willingness to learn. Also, this person was able to articulate a strength and be open about his or her reluctance to travel great distances at night. . . a picture of a healthy and honest person is emerging.)

I: What has been your experience in organizing people?

C: As a matter of fact, I presently volunteer at my daughter's grammar school in the library where I head up the "Literary Moms" who read to the various classrooms.

I: How do you organize them?

C: I schedule the times for the moms to work, and I help to organize the books according to age appropriateness. Also, at the end of the year, I plan a party for the moms. . .actually it's an appreciation luncheon, thanking them for their hard work and dedication as volunteers.

I: Is there anything you don't enjoy in this position?

C: For some reason, I don't like to make lots of phone calls. So sometimes I don't always do the necessary follow-up and have had to get a couple of moms to help me with that task.

(This person seems to have some good organizational skills and is able to lead a group and get a task done. Understands the need for affirmation; not good at follow-up; might need some help with that.)

In the above answers, the following qualities of the candidate can be ascertained:
—potential
—degree of enthusiasm
—desire to be on the board
—level of interest
—level of knowledge
—skills
—qualities the person would bring to the ministry of board member

In taking notes, retain the "important things" (as derived from job description) that are talked about and also something about the candidate's attitude during your discussion. These things are important if you are going to fairly represent this person to a board or whatever group will consider this individual.

train·ing

TO MAKE PROFICIENT WITH SPECIALIZED INSTRUCTION AND PRACTICE

Training is equipping an individual or group of persons with the knowledge and skills necessary for a particular task. Through training, the liturgy personnel of a parish become qualified to accomplish their goals. When training in liturgy and leadership is ignored, board members are less able to discuss, make decisions or set effective goals. Education and training won't solve all disagreements, but a solid knowledge will provide direction for all three areas.

Every member of the liturgy board, no matter how well he or she knows a particular ministry, needs a knowledge of liturgy as a whole. This overview of liturgy should include:

—the structure and flow of the eucharistic liturgy
—the liturgical year, the rituals and festivals that belong to each season
—a sense of each of the ministries and their interplay in serving the liturgy
—the role of music in the liturgy
—guidelines for environment and art

Why is education and training in these areas so necessary? Let's say that the board is evaluating the communion rite at Sunday Mass. The members will be unable to have a fruitful discussion unless the group shares an understanding of liturgical structure and of the ministries involved in the communion rite. Liturgy is not grounded in personal opinion, but in a rich tradition and evolving practice. It is unfair to the parish to entrust the liturgical leadership to those who rely only on personal opinion and well-liked practices rather than on our tradition and its current expression.

In addition to basic knowledge in liturgy, the board members need training in leadership skills. Those who are part of the liturgy board will need skills in running meetings, listening, writing, delegating and managing people. Some board members will bring these skills to their service on the board; others will need a willingness to learn. A blend of liturgical knowledge and leadership skills is essential for the best possible participation and effectiveness of the liturgy board. The training should include an orientation, especially when there is an existing board. This orientation should introduce members to the purpose and structure of the liturgy board and to each other.

Ongoing Training

Once board members have participated in some basic study of the liturgy and in some skill development techniques, they will feel more competent. However, such initial training will not enable them to continue their work indefinitely. Board members need to cultivate a *mature* understanding of liturgy and to sharpen their management and communication skills continually. The means of providing ongoing education are many: liturgy and/or leadership workshops, retreat days, individual reading, lectures, video presentations, and activities during meeting times.

In some of these training opportunities the whole group should take part. More than one member should ordinarily go to a workshop or conference. This increases the likelihood that the whole board and parish assembly will benefit from the new learning, and the dialogue between those attending will benefit them and the board as a whole. Rotating attendance at such events is important. Encourage those who attend to develop creative ways to share their experience with the board: visual aids, a brief presentation, role playing, or handouts from their notes.

A caution on handling new material from workshops: not everything will be appropriate for your parish. New learning can increase your awareness of how your parish is doing and provide direction for the parish's liturgical life. The liturgy board will need to decide the pace at which they can implement such change.

Training New Members

As new members are invited to the liturgy board and others move on, as new ministries are developed and are represented for the first time, training for newcomers is crucial. Before newcomers can participate comfortably and with confidence, most will need to catch up with the experienced board members. Simply attending meetings is not enough.

A liturgy board will be called on to train new members regularly. This can seem awkward if there are only one or two new members; here are some approaches to incorporating new members into an existing liturgy board:

—Sponsor a training event for new liturgy board members with neighboring parishes.
—If it has been two or three years since the initial training of the board, have everyone, experienced and newcomers, go through a training event together. This can be an excellent refresher and energizer. Experienced members can assist in facilitating small group discussion.
—Use any changes in liturgical practice that have been recommended as a springboard for individual reading and discussion.
—Pair a new member with an experienced member to talk about articles, other learning material, board meetings, etc.

Some of the above are minimal ways of learning what is necessary and they should be considered supplemental methods. However, they can provide variety. Such experiences also promote good relationships between parishes. If the material seems appropriate, sessions could also be offered to all the liturgical ministers and/or to the parish at large. The appropriate audience, of course, is determined by the content of the presentation.

How Training Is Done and by Whom

Following are a variety of opportunities; most require time and money and will need to be included in the budget.

1. Contact your diocesan office of worship to inquire about its resources and services. Is there a library of books, pamphlets and audio visual materials, a mailing list, workshops and seminars, newsletters? If your diocese has no liturgy office, find out why. Make it known that you need and would use one.
2. Request to be put on the mailing list of publishers of liturgical materials.
3. Subscribe to liturgy periodicals of good quality.
4. Combine your training efforts with nearby parishes that have similar needs.
5. Contact local high schools or colleges to explore what offerings they have in leadership training.
6. A community center or place of business may sponsor seminars in some areas of leadership or management.
7. Find out if people on the board have access to training materials (e.g., tapes, filmstrips, books, etc.) from their workplace.
8. Allow time at board meetings to include sharing from those who have been to a workshop.
9. If your diocese offers a lay ministry training program, find out about it. Is any of the training available to you?

10. Three or four times a year invite a speaker to help your group do an in-depth study of one area of liturgy.

Planning to Meet Your Education and Training Needs

Use *Training Worksheets 1* and *2* as planning resources to determine the background of the group in liturgy and in leadership. They will help you determine a focus for the group's needed education and training. If several board members have participated in workshops on communication, initial leadership training could be in another area, such as delegating or problem solving. If most of the group has attended workshops on the liturgical ministries, training might focus on the structure of the liturgy or historical background.

When contemplating the training/education of parish liturgy personnel (e.g., lectors, ushers, choir, etc.), use *Training Worksheet 3*. Involve all board members in deciding the content or format of training. Although we know that certain areas are essential, the group's needs or interests may suggest a focus. Group members are more likely to be willing to participate if they have had an opportunity to help design the training.

It is most helpful if someone on the board is charged with seeing to various facets of continuing education for the board itself and even for the various ministries and the larger parish. This board member would stay in close contact with the diocesan liturgy office to provide information on workshops, conferences and related events. Many diocesan offices publish newsletters. The office itself may have a good resource of liturgy publications. Part of this board member's charge would be to provide reading material relevant to the board's needs and interests.

Training Worksheet 1

1. List your formal and informal learning experiences in liturgy. This will help us discover our strengths as well as the areas in which we need training.

   Formal experiences: consider classroom situations, workshops, study programs.

   Informal: consider participation in good liturgy, periodicals, dialogue with knowledgeable people, keeping of rituals in your home, etc.

2. In what aspects of liturgy are you most knowledgeable or experienced?

3. What aspects of liturgy are you most interested in learning about? In what aspects do you need more training to fulfill your role?

Training Worksheet 2

1. List your formal and informal learning experiences in leadership and management. This will help us discover our strengths as well as the areas in which we need growth.

   Formal experiences: consider classroom situations, work place experiences, seminars, etc.

   Informal experiences: consider learning from such models as parents, teachers, supervisors; experience in parenting, chairing a committee or project, running a home.

2. In what aspects of leadership are you most skilled?

3. In what aspects of organization/communication/management do you want more skill?

Training Worksheet 3

(Use this worksheet to consolidate your plans to train parish liturgy personnel.)

1. **Based on the individual reports, what do we need to learn?**
   (Consider the knowledge needed to achieve your group's goals and the skills you already have or lack.)

2. **When will we provide training?**
   (Consider whether you can function without further training. How soon should training take place to help you achieve your goals?)

3. **Who will provide or facilitate the training?**
   (Consider resources within your parish, other resources in your diocese or neighboring dioceses, local college faculties, your budget.)

4. **Who will participate? To whom is this training event geared?**
   (New members of a liturgy board, existing board members, particular ministers, the assembly, the parish staff?)

For Further Study

The following are recommended for initial and continuing formation of those involved in parish liturgy:

Books about Liturgy

Bernardin, Joseph. *Guide for the Assembly.* Chicago: Liturgy Training Publications, 1997. A reprint of Cardinal Bernardin's pastoral letter, *Our Communion, Our Peace, Our Promise,* addressed to the assembly and inviting all to understand and take responsibility for the liturgy. Study notes and discussion guide are now included.

Fleming, Austin. *Preparing for Liturgy.* Chicago: Liturgy Training Publications, 1997. Fundamentals of why, how and who we worship. Both basic and profound reflection on our underlying attitudes about liturgy.

Foley, Edward. *From Age to Age: How Christians Have Celebrated the Liturgy.* Chicago: Liturgy Training Publications, 1991. Focusing on the music, books, vessels and architecture, Foley tells how Christians through the ages celebrated and understood their eucharist. Illustrated with quotations, photographs, maps, drawings and stories.

Huck, Gabe. *Liturgy with Style and Grace.* Chicago: Liturgy Training Publications, revised edition, 1998. A survey of the Mass, the ministries, the seasons and elements of ritual, arranged in two-page essays with reflection questions. A bibliography is included.

Kavanagh, Aidan. *Elements of Rite.* New York: Pueblo Publishing, 1982. Concise, wonderfully written confrontation with all we do wrong.

The Liturgy Documents. Chicago: Liturgy Training Publications, revised edition, 1991. The basic documents from Rome and the U.S. bishops (partial list): *Constitution on the Sacred Liturgy, General Instruction of the Roman Missal, Lectionary for Mass: Introduction, General Norms for the Liturgical Year and Calendar, Directory for Masses with Children, Music in Catholic Worship, Liturgical Music Today, Environment and Art in Catholic Worship.* Each document is preceded by a general overview that notes the origins, importance, strengths and weaknesses of the document.

Mahony, Cardinal Roger. *Gather Faithfully Together: Guide for Sunday Mass.* Chicago: Liturgy Training Publications, 1997. Cardinal Mahony sets out his vision of a parish Sunday eucharist, addressing the vigor of the Sunday assembly, its beauty and liveliness, quiet and passion.

White, James. *Introduction to Christian Worship.* Nashville: Abingdon Press, 1980. This volume is used as a text in many introductory college courses.

Periodicals

Assembly. Chicago: Liturgy Training Publications. Five times a year. Short but excellent essays that explore one aspect of liturgy in each issue.

Liturgy 90. Chicago: Liturgy Training Publications. Eight times a year. Short articles on a variety of topics, always including some of great usefulness in the parish.

National Bulletin on the Liturgy. Ottawa: Canadian National Liturgical Office. Five times a year. Each issue is a thorough treatment of a single subject. Many back issues available.

Pastoral Music. Washington: National Association of Pastoral Musicians. Six times a year. Music is central, but many related topics are treated; reviews and columns survey material of recent interest.

Worship. Collegeville: St. John's Abbey. Six times a year. Scholarly articles and reviews; the liturgical movement in the United States has been shaped and chronicled in these pages.

Plenty Good Room. Chicago: Liturgy Training Publications. Six times a year. A forum on the spirit and truth of African American worship in the Catholic church. Occasional book reviews and prayer service suggestions are also included.

PART 2: KEEPING IT TOGETHER

pro·ce·dure

A MANNER OF
PROCEEDING;
WAY OF
PERFORMING
OR EFFECTING
SOMETHING

Once job descriptions are in place and people have been recruited and trained, you have a liturgy board! So if you've made it this far, this accomplishment needs to be acknowledged and recognized by yourselves and by the parish. The tasks that follow take a tremendous amount of energy and commitment and would only be done by a group that has decided to accept the responsibility for liturgy in the parish. A celebration of what's been done so far is in order. Tell the assembly who you are and what you're about in the parish bulletin (or at a ritual of commissioning during a weekend liturgy). If your parish council has empowered and encouraged your development, this kind of ritual could take place at one of the council meetings.

When a liturgy board knows its purpose, has developed its job descriptions, and has recruited and trained members, it is time to state in a formal, written manner *how* the board will operate. If board members are ambiguous about their roles and relationships, disharmony and tension are likely to occur. A clear shared understanding of the procedures and roles helps board members feel secure ("We know how we do this!") and lessens their frustrations. Also, a concise statement of procedures increases the probability that expectations will be met. When people feel secure and enthusiastic about their involvement, they are better able to work together to meet the group's goals. Establishing procedures, of course, will not eliminate every problem—even dynamic groups will run into the unexpected and have to cope with it.

Once the board's procedures are agreed upon, they must be reviewed periodically. What is best for now may not meet tomorrow's needs. If the board is new, we suggest a review be in place within three to six months. For an established group, an annual review is sufficient.

When establishing procedures, each of the following elements should be considered.

Board Membership

Here you will name the positions on the liturgy board. This will depend on the structure of the board. Refer to Chapter 3, "Assessment."

Becoming a Board Member

Ideally, people are invited to become liturgy board members because they exhibit leadership potential, good communication skills, and fit the job description for their position (see "Recruitment"). Board members are sometimes a combination of elected and invited/appointed people. Where elections are held, we urge that the board itself establish a slate of suitable candidates who have the appropriate background and experience in liturgy. An at-large board is a poor method for a parish to acquire people skilled in liturgy.

Term of Commitment

Board members should serve a two- or three-year term. Such a term gives some stability to the board, encourages people to work and stay with the job, and allows them to choose other involvements at the end of that time. Two or three years is enough time to become comfortable and competent in a job and to enjoy some accomplishments.

Limiting the length of service can make a board look to others whose competence and enthusiasm would be an asset. Knowing that terms are limited encourages board members to educate more people in liturgy.

If you decide to choose a three-year term of commitment for ministry chairpersons, here is one style of involvement for the third year. Choose a replacement at the end of the second year using the steps outlined in the chapter on recruitment. The outgoing person remains for this third year and gradually prepares the new person. The person being trained could take on some of the tasks of that ministry, then assume the full role at the end of the year.

Responsibility for Ongoing Recruitment

We have already established that whoever gets this board in motion would deal with the initial recruitment. The entire board is charged with the responsibility for seeing that gradual replacement takes place smoothly.

When a chairperson is leaving a leadership role, he or she would be the most appropriate person to determine a replacement. The selection process would then be done by the entire group. Where a member-at-large is being replaced, everyone could participate in brainstorming names. In either situation, the steps that follow "Surfacing Names," in the chapter on recruitment, would be adapted to particular needs at this time. All new members should receive an orientation, a chance to discuss the job description, and the training described earlier.

Offices Necessary to Run the Board

The chairperson or liturgy coordinator must head the board, set the agenda, chair the meetings, and keep people on task. This person also supports co-workers and affirms their participation.

A method to record what happens at meetings and to provide a written group history—the minutes—is another necessity. This could be a volunteer from the parish who can attend the meetings and take notes, or arrange to tape the meetings and prepare the minutes later. It is best that a board member not act in this function.

Time and Place

Frequency, time and location of meetings should also be addressed in the liturgy board's procedures. The length of meetings may vary, but beginning and ending times should be clear beforehand. If board members are required to take part in a specified number of meetings per year, indicate that as well (see Chapter 9, "Agenda").

Who Makes Decisions

Not every decision about the liturgy can or should be made by the full board. Such a procedure would paralyze the actions of the ministry chairpersons. Normally, decisions are best made at the lowest possible level. For example, the lector chairperson should be able to decide who will provide a workshop for the lectors. The ability to make that kind of choice will evolve from adequate training and the experience of overseeing a ministry. When an entire board gets involved in details, everyone's energy is drained. Instead, promote respect and teamwork.

The board deals only with the broader decisions. To determine whether a decision is of such scope, ask how many people will be affected by the decision, ascertain if the decision will effect a permanent change or precedent, determine the size of the expense that may result from the decision.

How Decisions Are Made

Making decisions is best done by consensus: reaching agreements, solutions and goals that everyone can live with, although not everyone may agree with every part. Decisions take more work and more time this way, but the results will have a great deal of understanding and commitment behind them. Simple voting can be a divisive technique, especially when the group seems to be at an impasse. Calling for a vote most often polarizes a group into factions instead of forcing it to find a common ground.

If the board's decisions need to be approved by the pastor (or some other structure), the liturgy board needs to know that from the start and work within those boundaries.

Assuring Growth Experiences

Growth in liturgical knowledge and spirituality, growth in skills and relationships, is not likely to happen if left to chance. Decide from the start to plan and provide, at least once a year, an extended opportunity for the board to renew its energy and for board members to become more effective liturgical servants for the parish.

Discerning Effectiveness

Effectiveness is measured by evaluating the board's activities at predetermined intervals. Look at how the board is functioning, how the meetings are being run, how the liturgical seasons are kept, how the eucharistic liturgy is celebrated, how the ministers are functioning—everything that affects parish liturgy. This enables the liturgy board to move ahead in a responsible and thoughtful manner.

Working Relationships and Communications

The procedures discussed above are the groundwork of a liturgy board's operations. Another type of procedure has to do with establishing the patterns and channels of communication between the various groups and individuals, between the ministry chairpersons, and between the liturgy board and other parish groups.

To establish an effective working relationship, begin by identifying the roles of those whose work is related to the liturgy. A good deal of friction results when responsibility for a task or goal is unclear. Ask yourself whose interests, responsibilities and goals dovetail with yours. This may include the parish school, the peace and justice committee, the catechumenate team, hospital/homebound ministers, evangelization, youth ministry, etc. Ideally, the work of a well-functioning parish council includes creating the structure and climate for parish organizations to coordinate their work. If this is not the case, build those communication networks yourself. If all parish boards or committees have some sense of the focus and scope of others' work, they will have a better sense of when and how it is fitting to work together and will keep others informed of their own work.

As an example, suppose that the RCIA director wants to find a way to present the catechumens to the assembly during the Sunday liturgy. The RCIA director knows that liturgy teams are responsible for harmony between environment, music, gesture and text. The RCIA director will talk to the chairperson for overall preparation of Sunday liturgies during a season. The chairperson coordinates everyone responsible for preparation of the liturgy on a particular Sunday. What could have been an uncomfortable surprise—a last minute gesture thrown into an otherwise well-prepared liturgy—goes smoothly.

There are also times when the liturgy board needs to consult with other groups about its plans. If one of the goals of the liturgy board for the coming year is to provide liturgical education for the assembly, it would be wise to approach the education board. It may be discovered that the adult education committee was also considering a similar program prompted by parents' participation in children's liturgies and other sacramental celebrations. Such communication not only promotes good relationships, it also enables both liturgy board and adult education committee to share the tasks and expenses of implementing a common goal.

Always consider who might be interested in or need to know what you are doing, and who else may benefit from a particular project. Providing others with accurate information and opportunities to contribute to decisions is always worth the time and effort.

Sample Procedures for a Liturgy Board

Board Membership

The liturgy board of St. Luke's parish shall consist of: a paid liturgy coordinator; one representative of the following ministries: music, lectors, liturgy planning, environment and art, eucharistic ministers, ushers; a clergy representative; two representatives of the assembly. In the selection of the above representatives, the board will work to include a cross section of the assembly in terms of sex, age, ethnic origin, and participation in a particular liturgy.

Membership will be open to individuals who possess knowledge of liturgy or the willingness to be trained, leadership abilities or the willingness to be trained, and a sense of ritual celebration. Involvement in a liturgical ministry is preferred.

Members will agree to a two-year commitment with evaluation, three years maximum with evaluation.

New members will be required to attend initial training in the areas of liturgy and leadership.

Responsibility for recruitment of board members will be in the hands of the liturgy coordinator, who may enlist the assistance of the board and in particular the help of the member being replaced.

Structure and Meetings

Attendance on a regular basis is expected. After two consecutive unexplained absences, the coordinator will contact the member to determine the person's commitment.

The following position will be in place to facilitate the board's work: a person to take minutes.

The liturgy board will meet on the second Tuesday of each month except during December and July. Each meeting will begin with prayer, and approximately one-third of the time will be devoted to ongoing education for all members.

The board will attempt to decide issues by reaching consensus. In the event of an impasse, the chairperson may call for a vote. In this case, a quorum will consist of more than half the membership; a passing vote is three-fourths of those present. Visitors and substitutes for members may not vote.

Other Policies

The board will meet at least once a year for the purpose of spiritual and social growth.
The board will evaluate its structure, members, meetings and goals annually.
The work of this board will be defined in accordance with its job description.
The board will coordinate efforts with other parish organizations or functions as needed.

budg·et

THE TOTAL SUM OF MONEY ALLOCATED FOR A PARTICULAR PURPOSE OR TIME PERIOD

As a liturgy board, have you found yourself saying: "There never seems to be enough money to accomplish all we hope to do," or "How do I know how much I can spend on this project?" If so, the answer to your concerns may be found in the careful preparation of a yearly budget. Budgeting may not be everyone's favorite task, but it is necessary to keep expenses from outpacing parish resources. Having a budget has some advantages. First, a budget frees from uncertainty by providing the boundaries within which we can operate. Second, a budget can become a historical document that tells what tasks the board was about, what was needed and how much was spent. Third, a budget is invaluable for projecting financial needs and making plans. Finally, a budget gives the board and ministers a feeling of being responsible; that is, it affords them a clear sense of what they are able to spend and to accomplish.

If establishing a budget still seems overwhelming, and you remain unsure how to proceed, remember that people outside the liturgy board can often be of great help. For example, most parishes include people who are financial planners and/or accountants. Seek out these people to help you set up your budgeting system.

Once a budget is set and approved by the appropriate body in the parish, be clear about what procedures must be followed to spend the money and who may authorize expenditures. Some parish personnel want to assess every expenditure, while others only look at purchases over a certain dollar amount. Some will permit necessary spending as long as the budget is not exceeded. The key is communication. Know how things are handled in your parish and work within that framework. If your parish does not presently operate with a budget for liturgy, begin to work toward one. Responsible handling of monetary resources is another step toward responsible lay ministry. A budget is a means of consciously planning for parish priorities and will be a valuable tool even if funds generally are available for liturgical needs. While parishes usually have money designated for individual ministries, they often overlook planning an operational budget for the board itself. Be attentive in this regard.

Be sure the overall budget includes:

— a budget for those items necessary to the board's functioning (e.g., a copy of *The Liturgy Documents* for each member, postage, etc.)
— a budget for the maintenance and development of each ministry (e.g., stipends for outside speakers, cost of materials to train ministers)
— budgets to cover special projects for the year ahead (e.g., a day of formation for all ministers may require hiring a keynote speaker, workshop facilitators, refreshments, mailings, handouts, etc.)

Creating a New Budget

If the liturgy board is new or has never had the opportunity to develop a budget, you need to research what is needed to maintain the board and the various ministries. Seek out the people who can tell you what has been spent in the past. The lectors will know if they have been given a copy of *Workbook for Lectors* each year. The ministers of communion will know about their annual retreat day. Examine the parish ledger to see if line items are noted in detail for each ministry or major project. Ongoing expenses such as candles, palms, bread and wine for the eucharist should not be overlooked.

Finally, when shaping a new budget, it is always good to look to the wisdom of the group. Brainstorming for budget items with all the eucharistic ministers will help to see that nothing essential to their work is left out. We also recommend that ministry chairpersons work on, or at least review, their budgets together. Such cooperation not only creates camaraderie, but also increases understanding of one another's ministry. This, in turn, quiets any feelings of unfairness over the amount allocated to another ministry, develops a greater sense of ownership for the work of the liturgy, and lessens the monotony of the task.

You have probably realized by now the importance of training. Ideally, every ministry could have training available to them every year, but not every parish budget can support that kind of expenditure. So think about he possibility of sharing the available money from year to year. Begin by taking an honest look at how the ministries are functioning and who needs the most help. Maybe the lectors have had no training for three years but music has been given much attention for the last two. Could the lectors be given the training allowance this year for a training program and a speaker? Could the musicians skip a year?

Once the budget is determined through inquiry and brainstorming, it is then presented to the appropriate body for review, e.g., the parish council, a finance committee, or the pastor. If cuts are necessary, the liturgy board will need to re-evaluate what it hopes to accomplish in the coming year, especially if available funds will not cover the established goals. Don't go automatically to the ministry with the largest budget, nor simply cut all by a given percent. Rather, thoughtful reflection is needed. Remember that the official parish budget need not be the board's only source of funding. Other sources of support such as fund raisers, bequests and donations may also be available if allowed by parish policy. Be creative in your budgeting.

Working from an Existing Budget

Use the previous year's budget and list of expenses as a basis for preparing the coming year's budget. With that as a foundation, have the board ask itself the following questions:

— What were the actual expenses for the board and for each ministry?
— In what areas was the board over or under budget?
— Were the actual expenses more realistic than the budget?

If discrepancies are found, look at them closely. Perhaps the board or a particular ministry had too many goals for the year. Budgeting must always come after goal setting.

The worthiness of a budget cannot be read in its bottom line. When establishing a budget based on an existing one, make sure you do a thorough assessment of how well that existing budget has served you. Then make alterations for the coming year based not only on the past, but also on your goals for the future.

Setting the Budget

Whether you are working from an existing budget or creating a totally new one, use the *Budget Preparation Worksheet*. As a board, your final budget will be composed from a number of smaller budgets: namely, those of each ministry plus the operating budget of the board itself. It is best to start by establishing the budget for the board; this may eliminate duplication of items in the budgets of specific ministries.

Distribute copies of the *Budget Preparation Worksheet* to each board member.

Carefully go through the worksheet together. Record the list of proposed expenditures on chalkboard or paper. If discrepancies or disagreements occur, spend time to reach consensus on the expenditures necessary. Refer to the goals the board agreed to emphasize. Finally, using a copy of the *Budget Form*, list all items with a dollar amount. Make sure each board member has a copy of the completed *Budget Form*. To assist you in this task, see the *Sample Budget Preparation Worksheet* and the *Sample Budget Form*.

Direct each ministry chairperson to repeat the above procedure with regard to the budget needs of his or her liturgical ministry. If necessary, have each chairperson call a meeting of the ministers he or she represents to accomplish this task. Once each ministry has completed a *Budget Form*, gather the liturgy board together to review each budget and then to combine all—including the one for the board—into a final budget. When presenting the final budget to the appropriate parish body for review, be sure to attach copies of the goals and individual Budget Forms.

Budget Preparation Worksheet

Task: Look over the job description and goals of the board itself and each ministry for which you need to develop a budget. Decide what resources you need to fulfill those duties. Then brainstorm the areas for which expenditures will be needed. The categories given below may be useful.

Things Needed:	Training Expenditures:
Office Supplies:	**Miscellaneous:**

Sample Budget Preparation Worksheet

Task: Look over the job description and goals of the member and board itself and each ministry for which you need to develop a budget. Decide what resources you need to fulfill those duties. Then brainstorm the areas for which expenditures will be needed. The categories given below may be useful.

Things Needed:	Training Expenditures:
—magazine subscriptions — copy of The Liturgy Documents for each member	—speaker for in-service workshop —new books — funds for diocesan workshops
Office Supplies:	**Miscellaneous:**
—Stationery/envelopes — stamps — markers/newsprint —photocopy expenses	—refreshments/cups —funding for day of recollection

Budget Form

Budget for:

Year:

Last Year's Actual Expenses:

Last Year's Budget:

Things Needed:

Training Expenditures:

Office Supplies:

Miscellaneous:

Total Projected Budget:

Sample Budget Form

What follows is a sample budget for the needs of the liturgy board. It does not include what is needed for each ministry, salaries, or what needs to be purchased to promote good liturgy in the parish. The total parish liturgy budget would include all these things.

Budget for: St. Mary's Liturgy Board (12 members)

Year: 1988/1989

Last Year's Actual Expenses: $937.00

Last Year's Budget: $950.00

Things Needed:
12 copies of *The Liturgy Documents* @ 6.00/$72.00
 2 pads of newsprint @ 11.50 each/23.00

Training Expenditures:
allowance for possible new resource/100.00
allowance for in-service speaker/125.00
allowance to send members to up-coming workshops, etc./200.00

Office Supplies:
postage/40.00
paper (folders, stationary, envelopes, etc.)/50.00
pens, pencils, markers/15.00
photocopying on parish machine at .02 per copy/20.00

Miscellaneous:
allowance for a day of recollection/200.00
refreshments and paper goods for meetings, training sessions
and recruitment sessions, etc./150.00

Total Projected Budget: 995.00
Allowance for emergencies etc./99.00
1094.00
1100.00 (rounded)

a•gen•da

A LIST OF
THINGS TO BE
DONE,
ESPECIALLY THE
PROGRAM FOR
A MEETING

Agendas help groups accomplish those things that have been agreed upon as important. For a liturgy board, the agenda grows out of its goals and job description. Translating the duties given in the job description into an agenda ensures good use of meeting time and keeps the board working toward its goals throughout the year. By setting agendas, the board avoids addressing the same things over and over again with the frustration that entails. The liturgy board must concern itself with two types of agendas: a yearly agenda and a meeting agenda.

The liturgy board should prepare a yearly agenda to assure that goals will be addressed throughout the year. To begin, decide when "a year" begins and ends. Then look at those things on the job description that need attention this year: is it goal setting, evaluating seasonal liturgies, preparing the budget? Some of these agenda items will demand attention at a particular time during the liturgical year or be determined by events on the parish calendar. For example, lenten liturgies should be evaluated soon after Easter. Likewise, if the parish finance committee approves budgets in June, the board will need to do its financial planning in April or May. Goal setting will have to be completed if the budget is to include what is necessary to meet the goals. Other items, such as ongoing training or evaluating a part of the

Sunday liturgy, can be addressed at any time of the year.

While preparing the yearly agenda, continue to refer to the job description to make sure that the board has time to address its major duties each year. If this proves impossible, be sure to carry over missed items into the following year's agenda. Recognize that some things on the yearly agenda may be part of the parish's long-range plans (e.g., a five year plan for liturgy). Thus, if the parish has decided to hire a liturgy coordinator within the next three to five years, the liturgy board may develop the job description this year, but wait until the following to recruit.

It is better to take on fewer tasks and accomplish them than to take on too much and fail. Always consider the present resources and abilities of the group or parish. As you set your yearly agenda, use the *Sample Annual Agenda* as a guide to help you in your task.

The Meeting Agenda

The second type of agenda with which a liturgy board must concern itself is the meeting agenda. Too often meetings that last three hours accomplish very little. Such situations can be avoided when liturgy board members know what is to be included in their meetings, who will prepare the agenda, what material will be needed to participate, and how the meeting will be handled.

In deciding *what* to include in a meeting, we suggest that each meeting deal with at least one item from the yearly agenda, and that it be the major agenda item for the meeting. If a special project or unexpected situation needs attention, include that on the agenda as well. We strongly suggest that every meeting also include ongoing education, prayer, evaluation, and a brief socializing activity. These things meet the diverse needs of board members, and thus enable them to get the work done.

Someone needs to be responsible for preparing the agenda and distributing it to the members at least a week in advance for review and preparation. This task can be performed by the board's chairperson. A helpful addition to the agenda is a written report from each ministry chairperson when necessary. Extensive reporting during the meetings takes valuable time; keeping in touch with the progress of the liturgical ministries can be easily done through a written report that is included with the agenda and read before the meeting. During the meeting, time can be allotted for questions and clarification of the reports. Accomplishments should be publicly recognized.

When deciding the order of agenda items, it is important to know the group. Do they prefer to address the major task at the beginning of the meeting? Are they refreshed by prayer at the beginning and better able to address the work after that experience? Are they unable to be attentive to ongoing education at the end of the meeting? However the agenda is ordered, it is important that it be owned by the group. This means providing an opportunity to adjust or add to the agenda for items of immediate concern.

When planning meeting agendas, the following are some things to avoid:

—running over the time allowed for the meeting without the group's agreement
—working on the details that belong in subcommittees or a ministry group
—using the meeting to work out interpersonal conflicts
—extensive reports

A useful agenda is one that helps the liturgy board work toward its goals and accomplish its job in the time alotted.

A final but crucial item regarding agendas for meetings is the time meetings are held. Most meetings of church committees are held on weekday evenings for two or three hours. If that works well for you, carry on. However, sometimes this is not enough time to accomplish the work. If you find that people are too tired at day's end to concentrate on the tasks at hand, consider Saturday morning meetings. Depending on the availability of the board members, late afternoon may be another alternative. You might even consider an all-day session, especially if board members would prefer to work hard and complete a major goal rather than deal with it over several two-hour meetings. Regardless of when you meet or the length of the meeting, you need to ask yourselves: "Are we accomplishing our agenda and getting the job done?" If not, the group must consider other options rather than stay in an unproductive routine. Sometimes taping a meeting and listening to it later will reveal the problem. At other times, a skilled outsider can be asked to observe and make suggestions. In either case, the group's permission should be obtained.

Use a copy of the agenda worksheet to help plan your regular meetings. Check the filled-in *Sample Agenda* as a guide to help you complete your own.

Sample Annual Agenda

The following agenda reflects the goal setting of St. Perpetually Ready parish. The liturgy board has a number of standing committees which also meet regularly, but much less formally, to perform the necessary groundwork. This committee work leaves the board free to deal with the larger issues, especially the concerns which affect all ministries at once such as budgets and an annual calendar.

This coming year the board has decided to focus on two pressing needs: the improvement of parish weddings and the need for hospitality, a need which became apparent while evaluating the gathering rites of Sunday Mass the previous year. The board has decided to spend the year concentrating on these two areas, but at the same time to keep up with the work of the various standing committees. Since the demands of hospitality and weddings affect all ministries, no one ministry can deal adequately with these areas.

The board meets monthly, beginning its year in July. Every meeting includes 20 minutes of education in response to requests from board members, but sometimes 40 minute education sessions have been worked into the annual agenda. The board has a party in January, and parish organizations do not meet during Lent. In February the board holds an all-day session with the finance committee, board of education and parish council. Regular meetings are from 7:30-9:30 on week nights. In May (Eastertime) a weekend barbecue is planned for all liturgical ministers, and in June a Ministry Day is held.

JULY Present summary of last year's work in assessing the gathering rite of Sunday liturgy. Form committee to assess parish weddings.

AUGUST Hold education session about parish weddings. Midyear budget reports. Discuss overall board structure.

SEPTEMBER Hold education session about ministry of hospitality. Discuss report from parish wedding committee.

OCTOBER Form committee to organize Ministry Day for next June. Make recommendations regarding report from parish wedding committee. Discuss both past year's progress in improving the gathering rite and the pressing need for ministers of hospitality.

NOVEMBER Iron out problems with recommendations regarding parish weddings. Discuss large number of complaints in previous years about the efforts of the environment and art committee. Prepare annual calendar for final approval in February.

DECEMBER Progress report on parish weddings from committee. Special session for education about Advent/Christmastime. Preliminary budget discussion.

JANUARY Annual wine and cheese party.

FEBRUARY Special all-day Saturday meeting to finalize budgets and calendar, held with parish council and finance committee.

Sample Annual Agenda, continued.

MARCH No meeting during Lent. Parishioners meet weekly through Lent for prayer and discussion.

APRIL Progress report on June Ministry Day. Progress report from parish wedding committee. Form committee to organize ministry of hospitality.

MAY Iron out details for upcoming Ministry Day. Finalize a parish wedding policy based on year-long work of parish wedding committee. (An Eastertime barbecue is held on a weekend for all liturgical ministers, including all members of committees and board members.)

JUNE Progress report on newly-forming ministry of hospitality. Based on decisions regarding calendar and budgets, organize next year's agenda.

Agenda

Name of group:

Date and time of meeting:

Kind of meeting (circle one): quarterly, monthly, emergency/unscheduled, special focus, other _____

Chairperson/facilitator:

Prayer prepared by:

Educational component (describe, including any preparation to be done before the meeting):

Please read or bring:

Major agenda item:

Desired outcome:

Processes involved (for example, brainstorming, problem-solving, goal-setting, evaluating, etc.):

Other agenda items:

Refreshments provided by:

Sample Agenda

Name of group: St. Perpetually Ready Board

Date and time of meeting: 1/12/87, 7:00-9:30

Kind of meeting: (circle one) quarterly, (monthly) emergency/unscheduled, special focus, other _____

(Chairperson)/facilitator: Michael Stein

Prayer prepared by: Alice Jordan

Educational component (describe, including any preparation to be done before the meeting):
discussion of article on Liturgical Gestures, Assembly

Please read or bring:
the above article

Major agenda item:
evaluate liturgies of the Advent and Christmas seasons

Desired outcome:
articulate and record what went well; what needs improvement

Processes involved (for example, brainstorming, problem-solving, goal-setting, (evaluating,) etc.):
sharing input from evaluation forms

Other agenda items: _____

Refreshments provided by: Stan Lovett

e·val·u·a·tion

THE PROCESS OF EXAMINING OR JUDGING CAREFULLY

Periodic, systematic evaluation is necessary to ensure continued growth. Evaluation permits the liturgy board to affirm and applaud its accomplishments and to examine any problem areas. This kind of input enables thoughtful and intentional efforts toward change. In this sense, evaluation is vital to the board's success.

Evaluation also increases a sense of belonging by helping people to assess their individual strengths and weaknesses and to measure the effectiveness of the group. Thus, evaluation becomes the foundation for setting realistic goals for the liturgy board, the individual ministries and the parish liturgy. Records of the evaluations can provide a sense of progress and also a way for new members and chairpersons to become aware of their history.

Like any organization, a liturgy board can become ineffective but be uncertain of what is causing the difficulty. Evaluation is a way to find out. Regular and honest assessment—once a year for ongoing groups, every three to six months for a newly formed board—is essential. It will:

—assist board members in determining if their purpose is being enabled or disabled by the way they operate

—help the board feel good about its achievements in specific areas

—show the board where it must work to develop even more competence and productivity

The first *Evaluation Form* offers an opportunity for reflection on all areas of the board's work: its meetings, structure, goals, agenda, operational procedures, etc. You probably won't want to use your meeting for this work since it is time-consuming. All members should take one home with a clear understanding of where and when they are to return it. The liturgy coordinator or chairperson should be responsible for compiling the information and presenting the results to the board at a regular meeting.

How can this form be helpful? Problems raised under the heading "Operational Procedures" might suggest revisions that would address the board's goals. Positive comments regarding the yearly agenda indicate that the group has been effective in that area. This evaluation will clearly answer the question, "How are we doing?" and move the group forward in an orderly and purposeful manner.

Evaluating Individuals

Evaluating the chairperson, paid or volunteer staff, board members and ministry chairpersons affords an opportunity to see if the duties of the job descriptions are being carried out efficiently. Thus, reviewing the job description is always the first step before attempting to fill out the evaluation form. Such an evaluation is never done in isolation. Each member fills out a form, and the person to whom a board member reports, (coordinator, board chairperson, staff person) fills out an identical form. This method insures a fair discussion stemming from a common set of questions when the two come together for a review session. It is more than likely that many similar answers will appear. Any divergent responses will signal a need for more thorough discussion. For example, there may be a noticeable discrepancy between answers in the area of tasks not completed. This might be an indication of insufficient dialogue between two individuals over the past year. Is the chairperson or coordinator knowledgeable of what is being accomplished? Are expectations clear on both sides? Is the job description adequate or perhaps cluttered?

This evaluation should take place once a year to be of any real assistance. For a new member, an evaluation at three month intervals for the first year can prevent a minor difficulty from becoming a major issue. The evaluation works best when it is viewed as a concrete and constructive means of insuring that a job gets done well, and that this job meets the needs of the individual. Of course, placed in the wrong hands, the procedure could be divisive. It is not intended as a way to manipulate the membership merely on a basis of personality. When the form is used correctly it can help individuals set realistic goals, help them achieve the level of effectiveness they desire and show them their strengths and liabilities in leadership roles.

Evaluating a Liturgical Ministry

Someone has been assigned primary responsibility for developing and maintaining each ministry. These chairpersons are going to need input from their ministers to set goals for the following year and determine changes that would serve the ministry. The evaluation form provides such input as well as a tool for self-evaluation.

Evaluation of each ministry is appropriate once a year. The chairperson would be responsible for distributing the evaluation form to each minister with a schedule and method for return. It would be useful for the chairperson to keep these records on file to assist with long-range planning or provide smooth transition to a new chairperson.

The comments on these forms may serve as the basis for discussion at a meeting of ministers. The chairperson should summarize the comments and give them to each minister in advance of the meeting.

Evaluating a Liturgical Rite

Look at the liturgy as it is done on any given Sunday during Ordinary Time. Rather than evaluate everything within the liturgy at once, it may be more effective to choose a single rite (such as gathering or communion) and comment on the following items for that part of the Mass: ministers; gesture/ritual movement; music, symbols and objects. Over a length of time designated by the group, this method of evaluating enables the board to assess each of these things as they relate to and affect the way liturgy is done in the parish. Some things may be good in one moment of the liturgy and need improvement in another. Before an evaluation of a given rite, there might be a presentation or background reading and discussion on that part of the liturgy. Such education becomes the basis for each member's comments.

The board may proceed with this evaluation at whatever pace is permitted by its tasks and goals. A liturgy coordinator or chairperson would distribute an evaluation form once the group has decided on a particular part of the Mass or ministry. He or she would state a definite return date, allowing sufficient time to observe various liturgies and record comments. The results of these evaluations would be compiled and given to members to study before discussion by the group. This process highlights areas that need attention. Recommendations can then be made to the various ministries. These suggested improvements would become goals of the liturgy board or individual ministries.

Evaluating the Seasons

Another important task of the liturgy board is to evaluate the liturgical seasons. Refer to *Groundwork: Planning Liturgical Seasons* (LTP) for an evaluation form.

Evaluating the Board Meetings

Running an orderly, productive meeting requires learning and practice. Take five minutes at the end of each meeting for all present to evaluate the session. The evaluation form provides the necessary feedback for both the beginning and experienced chairperson. It can provide comments on the content or focus of the meeting as well as frequency of meetings and the structure of the agenda.

While this could be accomplished by a verbal "go-around-the-table," such sharing is sometimes less than completely candid. Once the chairperson has an opportunity to look over the evaluations, it would be helpful to share them with the board's staff liaison to determine where there is need to adjust the way meetings are planned and facilitated. An isolated negative comment should not be distressing. A pattern of comments from meeting to meeting is cause for concern. This evaluation also invites articulation of those things that are going well.

Evaluation Form
The Liturgy Board

MEETINGS

1. Comment on the number and frequency of meetings.

2. Does the present day/time slot fit your schedule? If not, suggest alternatives.

PRESENT STRUCTURE: Evaluate the adequacy of the number of people and positions in terms of effectiveness.

1. Consider the number of people on the board.
   too few   enough   too many

2. Consider the positions on the board.
   Are all liturgical ministries/staff represented?

   Are there enough positions to carry out duties and complete goals?

GOALS: Evaluate progress.

1. At what stage of accomplishment is each goal?

2. What is helping us to accomplish our goals?

3. What hinders progress?

The Liturgy Board (continued)

YEARLY AGENDA: Look at what needs to be done each year.

1. What was accomplished?

2. What was not? Why?

3. How and when might these tasks be addressed?

TRAINING: Evaluate content, facilitator, materials, opportunity for discussion.

1. What were the strengths of initial training?

—in liturgy?

—in leadership?

2. What were the weaknesses?

—in liturgy?

—in leadership?

3. What would be an improvement?

—in liturgy?

—in leadership?

The Liturgy Board (continued)

4. Is ongoing training being addressed?

5. Did this training take place at appropriate times? Comment.

6. Comment on the training's usefulness for our work.

COMMUNICATION: Take a look at how we communicate with each other, with staff, and with other parish boards/groups.

1. What has helped our communication with staff?

    What hindered? How can it be improved?

2. What has helped our communication with other parish boards/groups?

    What hindered? How can it be improved?

3. What are some effective ways we communicate with each other?

    What could be improved?

The Liturgy Board (continued)

4. What has helped to raise awareness of our function in the parish at large?

What hindered? How can it be improved?

DECISION MAKING: Evaluate the effectiveness of our method of making decisions.

1. How does our method move us along in our decision making?

2. In what ways does it prevent progress?

3. Is someone dominant? Is someone not participating?

The Liturgy Board (continued)

OPERATIONAL PROCEDURE: Consider the way our operational procedure works.

1. What supports and enables the work of the group?

2. What stifles the work?

3. What might need revision in light of the present duties and goals of the board?

GROWTH: Consider the ways in which the board has been attentive to the needs of its members.

1. What has been provided for educational growth?

    Suggestions:

2. What has been provided for spiritual growth?

    Suggestions:

3. What has been provided for social growth?

    Suggestions:

Evaluation Form
Board Members, Chairpersons and Staff

Name: _____

Position: _____

Year: _____

Carefully review the tasks which are covered in the job description.

1. List what you see as the four primary tasks of this job. Place a check mark by those that were completed.

2. List three of your significant accomplishments that relate to your present job description.

3. Of the four primary tasks listed in item 1, which were not accomplished this year? What prevented their completion? When and how will they be addressed?

    Are there other tasks which were not taken care of this year? What prevented their completion? When and how will they be addressed?

Board Members, Chairpersons and Staff (continued)

4. List the three greatest strengths that you bring to this job.

5. List three things you could improve during the next year to facilitate this ministry (or serve on this board).

6. List a specific goal to help you better serve your colleagues during the coming year.

Evaluation Form

Liturgical Ministry

Area of ministry: _____

Year: _____

Name: (optional) _____

1. List 1 to 3 things that are going well in this ministry.

2. List 1 to 3 things that need improvement in this ministry.

3. Comment on the usefulness of any training (initial/ongoing) and any resource materials (books, articles or periodicals) you received this year.

4. Comment on the present method of scheduling. Consider when schedules are being distributed and the weight given to ministers' preferences.

Liturgical Ministry (continued)

5. Comment on communication with the chairperson of this ministry. Consider availability, willingness to listen, frequency and style of communicating, ability to affirm.

6. What would help your competence in this area of service? Suggestions for:

   training

   spiritual growth

   socializing

   other

7. What expectations do you have of the ministry chairperson and the liturgy board or staff of the parish in relation to this ministry.

8. Other comments or suggestions for this ministry.

Evaluation Form
Liturgical Rite

Rite: _____

Date: _____

MINISTERS

1. Consider who needs primary involvement in this rite. Are the necessary ministers functioning?

2. In what ways are the ministers effective? What could be improved? Consider those things which help or hinder the people's prayer (e.g., the ministers' prayerfulness, appearance, skill or manner).

GESTURE/RITUAL MOVEMENT

1. Consider the appropriate gestures for this moment in the liturgy. Comment on how they are being done. Do they appear well coordinated? Are they done in a deliberate, thoughtful manner? Are they abrupt? Are they minimal or ample? Are they visible to the assembly? Should they be?

2. What contributes to the gracefulness and prayerfulness of these gestures or movement?

   What hinders?

3. Were the official options considered for this rite?

MUSIC

1. Is music called for at this part in the liturgy? Is it being used now?

Liturgical Rite (continued)

2. Comment on the appropriateness of the selection. Did it contribute to or interrupt the flow of the liturgy?

3. Is there an overload of music within the rite?

4. Do the texts and the melodies challenge us and reflect a mature faith?

5. Do the choices enable the participation of the assembly?

SYMBOLS AND LITURGICAL OBJECTS

1. Consider the objects or symbols used during this moment. Comment on the following:

Does this parish have the necessary liturgical equipment?

Are objects and symbols used appropriately?

Are they visible to the assembly? Consider their placement and size.

2. List suggestions for what needs to be purchased or crafted for use during this moment.

What could be discarded?

Evaluation Form
Liturgy Board Meetings

5 = done well
1 = done poorly

1. Keeping within the agenda

      5   4   3   2   1

2. Keeping on focus during discussion

      5   4   3   2   1

3. Getting through the agenda

      5   4   3   2   1

4. Participation by each group member

      5   4   3   2   1

5. Assisting in the accomplishment of goals

      5   4   3   2   1

6. One thing I learned at this meeting:

7. One thing I liked about this meeting:

8. One thing I think we accomplished:

a•men

AN EXPRESSION

OF

CONVICTION

OR ASSENT

Congratulations!

Depending on where you were as a group when you began this process (maybe a group didn't even exist), it has probably taken you anywhere from several months to a year and a half to be able to say a hearty AMEN. We congratulate you for staying with a project of such complexity and scope. For many of you, the organizational development process was new, something not readily associated with church and ministry.

Like you, we love our work in parish liturgy, but we also know the hurts and disappointments, the tedious hours that go along with the accomplishments. You probably never want to hear the words "job description" again! Right now you're hoping that your operational procedure will not need revision for a long time. But when you look around the meeting table and see enthusiastic board members who actually know why they are there, you experience a sense of accomplishment and pride. Do take the time to sit back, to feel good about what you've done and to celebrate—you deserve it! This is the time for all of you to make much of who you are and the important work you are about. Wherever you are, read on and discover how you can nurture yourself and each other, so that you may be about the work of the Lord.

Nurturing

Nurturing a group means developing a structure that accomplishes goals and meets the needs of its members. One of the ways a liturgy board can nurture relationships and replenish energies is to involve its members in activities that promote educational, spiritual and social growth. Such events should take place away from the work space. Create an environment that allows for hospitality, listening, rejoicing. Education can energize the group and give it the confidence to move forward. Socializing (e.g., through meals together and storytelling) helps people release the tensions that often arise with demanding work. Prayer can be a source of strength, peace, humility—forming us as we must be formed little by little into those who have put on Christ.

At meetings, prayer can be as brief as a scripture verse and silence or the Lord's Prayer, or it can be longer, perhaps the full but simple ritual of evening prayer.

Affirmation

What seems to be a lack of enthusiasm and energy due to overwork is often a symptom of a group's inability to affirm one another. Staff persons must provide affirmation to chairpersons. They, in turn, must affirm the ministers they serve. Encourage ministers to recognize the efforts of chairpersons and chairpersons to affirm the work of the parish staff. Each member needs to affirm others and to be the recipient of applause! Such affirmation need not be elaborate, expensive or overly frequent, but it should be more than a yearly event or an occasional thank you.

You can affirm by sending notes, by seeking out people at gatherings, by making phone calls. One lector chairperson calls her new lectors the night before they lector for the first time, attends the Mass at which they serve, then calls them during the week to go over how it went. When a group completes a job such as decorating the church for Christmas or sewing a new lectionary cover, consider giving them recognition in the parish bulletin. This attention to people's needs and abilities will greatly affect the attitudes and productivity of your liturgy board. Be careful of seeing others only in light of church work. Recognize the whole person: jobs and families and interests other than church. Be there for others—and not just for committee work.

Summary Comments

Some of you are encouraged by your progress in this process and some are discouraged. Some may have to be patient for a while. This may not be the best time to get started, but you care about your parish and the liturgy. Move ahead slowly, gaining support for this process from others.

You will probably need to refer to some part of this book again. Each year you will address the task of preparing budgets, setting an agenda, training, evaluating. At regular intervals the liturgy board will assess, perhaps revise, written procedure. If you decide to restructure the model you've chosen or to build on the one you now have, begin with assessment again and work through the necessary steps.

We hope this book will help you in your continuing efforts.

Other resources from Liturgy Training Publications:

Documents Books

The Liturgy Documents: A Parish Resource edited by Elizabeth Hoffman

Los Documentos Litúrgicos: Un Recurso Pastoral edited by Miguel Arias

The Liturgy Documents Vol. 1 on Disk for Windows

The Catechetical Documents: A Parish Resource edited by Martin Connell

Parish Approach to Liturgy

A Common Sense for Parish Life edited by Gabe Huck

Making Parish Policy: A Workbook on Sacramental Policies by Ron Lewinski

The Hardest Job: Leading a Parish to Live from its Liturgy (video)

Gather Faithfully Together: Guide for Sunday Mass by Cardinal Roger Mahony

We Gather in Christ: Our Identity as Assembly by the Worship Office of the Archdiocese
    of Cincinnati

General Preparation

Sourcebook for Sundays and Seasons by Peter J. Scagnelli

Prayers for Sundays and Seasons – Years A, B and C by Peter J. Scagnelli

To Crown the Year: Decorating the Church through the Seasons by Peter Mazar

The Sacristy Manual by G. Thomas Ryan

Basics of Ministry Series

Guide for Sponsors by Ron Lewinski

Guide for the Assembly by Cardinal Joseph Bernardin

Guide for Ushers and Greeters by Lawrence E. Mick

Video Guide for Ministers of Communion (video)

Guide for Ministers of Communion

Guide for Lectors

Guide for Choir Members

Guide for Sacristans

About the Mass

The Sunday Mass Video Series

The Roman Catholic Mass Today: Introduction and Overview (video)

We Shall Go Up with Joy: The Entrance Rite (video)

The Word of the Lord: The Liturgy of the Word (video)

Lift Up Your Hearts: The Eucharistic Prayer (video)

Say Amen! To What You Are: The Communion Rite (video)

The Communion Rite at Sunday Mass by Gabe Huck
The Eucharistic Prayer at Sunday Mass by Richard McCarron
The Dilemma of Priestless Sundays by James Dallen
Saving Signs, Wondrous Words by David Philippart
Preaching about the Mass by Gabe Huck

About the Sacraments

Infant Baptism: A Parish Celebration by Timothy Fitzgerald
New Life: A Parish Celebrates Infant Baptism (video)
Celebrating the Rites of Adult Initiation: Pastoral Reflections edited by Victoria Tufano
This Is the Night: A Parish Welcomes New Catholics (video)
Confirmation: A Parish Celebration by Timothy Fitzgerald
Eucharist as a Sacrament of Initiation by Nathan D. Mitchell
Removing the Barriers: The Practice of Reconciliation by James Dallen and Joseph Favazza
Parish Weddings by Austin Fleming

Canon Law

Disputed Questions in the Liturgy Today by John M. Huels, OSM
More Disputed Questions in the Liturgy by John M. Huels, OSM
The Catechumenate and the Law by John M. Huels, OSM

Administration

Schedule Maker for Liturgical Ministries (Version 6.0 for IBM compatible computers)
Clip Notes for Church Bulletins Volume 1 compiled and edited by Kathy Luty and David Philippart
Clip Art for Years A, B and C by Steve Erspamer, SM
Religious Clip Art for the Liturgical Year on Disk (for Windows and Macintosh) by Steve Erspamer, SM
Image America: The Image Book edited by Robert Kraay

Liturgy Training Publications, 1800 North Hermitage Avenue, Chicago IL 60622-1101;
1-800-933-1800; fax 1-800-933-7094.